Discover & Learn

British History

Teacher Book — Years 3-6

This Teacher Book accompanies CGP's Discover & Learn
British History books for Years 3-6.

It includes background information to help teachers
introduce and teach each topic, answers to every
question and plenty of suggestions for extra activities.

It's the perfect guide to planning and delivering
British History lessons throughout Key Stage Two!

Contents

Stone Age to Celts

History and Prehistory 1
How We Discover Prehistory 2
The First People in Britain 3
Early Humans in Britain 4
Life in the Glacial Periods 5
The Mesolithic 6
Life in the Mesolithic 7
Changes in the Mesolithic 8
The Neolithic 9
Neolithic Village Life 10
Neolithic Stone Circles 11
Flint, Copper and Bronze 12
Life After the Stone Age 13
Bronze Age Travel and Trade 14
Life in the Bronze Age 15
The End of the Bronze Age 16
The Celtic Age of Iron 17
Life in the Iron Age 18
An Invasion from Rome 19

Romans in Britain

The Romans Invade Britain 20
Trading and Invading 21
Britain Between the Caesars 22
Calleva Atrebatum 23
Claudius the Conqueror 24
The Roman Army 25
Building Roads to Conquer 26
The Invasion Continues 27
Turning Britain into Rome 28
Boudica Bites Back 29
Towards Scotland 30
Building Hadrian's Wall 31
Life at the Edge of the Empire 32
The Roman North 33
Living Like a Roman 34
Living in Luxury Villas 35
Religion in Roman Britain 36
Trouble in the Empire 37
The Romans Retreat 38

Anglo-Saxons

The Fall of the Roman Empire	39
The Romans Leave Britain	40
Writing About Britain	41
Life After the Romans	42
The First Invasions	43
Britain Fights Back	44
Becoming Anglo-Saxon	45
Anglo-Saxon Settlements	46
Daily Life for Anglo-Saxons	47
Anglo-Saxon Religions	48
Anglo-Saxon Law	49
The Top of Society	50
Beowulf and Sutton Hoo	51
The Bottom of Society	52
Anglo-Saxon Women	53
Anglo-Saxon Children	54
The Anglo-Saxon Kingdoms	55
The Golden Age	56
Defending Against Invaders	57

Vikings

Who Were The Vikings?	58
Viking Values	59
Norse Beliefs	60
Viking Voyages	61
Raiding and Trading	62
Viking Visits	63
Violent Vikings?	64
More Viking Visits	65
Viking Victories	66
Defeating the Anglo-Saxons	67
Alfred the Great	68
The Danes and the Danelaw	69
Viking Jorvik	70
Athelstan and Constantine	71
Vikings in the 10th Century	72
Aethelred is Unready!	73
King Canute and Emma	74
The Kings After Canute	75
The Conqueror is Coming	76

Published by CGP

Contributor: Joanna Copley

Editors: Andy Cashmore, Alex Fairer, Catherine Heygate, Kat Parkes

With thanks to Tom Carney and Maxine Petrie for the proofreading.

With thanks to Jan Greenway for the copyright research.

When using the Extra Activities in this product, please take the safety of the participants into consideration at all times, and ensure that children are supervised when researching material for this product online. Teachers should also take into account pupils' personal circumstances when dealing with topics of a sensitive nature.

ISBN: 978 1 78294 977 0

Printed by Elanders Ltd, Newcastle upon Tyne

Text, design, layout and original illustrations © Coordination Group Publications Ltd. (CGP) 2018
All rights reserved.

Photocopying more than 5% of this book is not permitted, even if you have a CLA licence.
Extra copies are available from CGP with next day delivery • 0800 1712 712 • www.cgpbooks.co.uk

History and Prehistory

Study Book (pages 2-3)

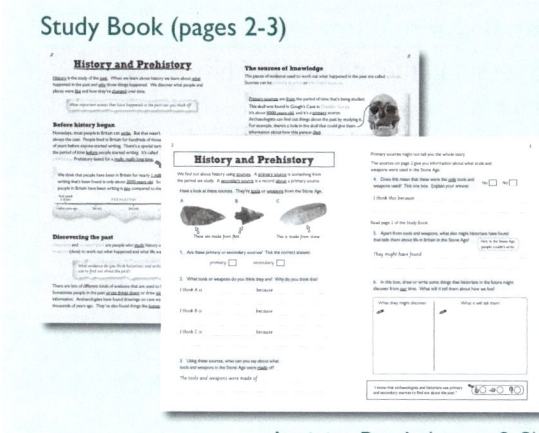

Activity Book (pages 2-3)

National Curriculum Aims

- Understand the methods of historical enquiry.
- Understand how evidence is used to make historical claims.
- Understand why there are different interpretations of the past.

Introduction

This topic will develop pupils' understanding of primary and secondary sources, and help them explore how historians interpret prehistoric sources. Ask pupils to think of things that could serve as primary sources (e.g. excavated artefacts, diaries, interviews) or secondary sources (e.g. textbooks, documentaries, biographies) and make two lists on the board. As a class, discuss the sorts of primary sources archaeologists might be able to find from the prehistoric period. Explain that sources from this period are rare and limited — a lot of the sources we would find useful from other eras (especially written and oral accounts) simply don't exist.

Answers to Activity Book Questions

1. Pupils should have ticked: primary.

2. E.g. *I think A is* an arrowhead *because* it's got a sharp, pointy end.
   I think B is an arrowhead *because* it's shaped to a sharp point and has a bit that you could attach wood to.
   I think C is an axe *because* it's got a sharp edge but looks heavy.

3. *The tools and the weapons were made of* flint and stone.

4. No. E.g. *I think this because* there might be tools or weapons that didn't survive or that haven't been discovered yet.

5. E.g. *They might have found* bones / clothes / drawings on cave walls / carved pictures. Do not accept references to written sources.

6. E.g. clothes — what we wore / cars — that we drove around /
   toys — what we played with / bones — what our bodies were like.

Extra Activities

- Show pupils a clip from the TV news. Is it a primary or a secondary source? As a class, discuss whether it shows society as pupils would want it to be remembered. Is it truly representative of life in Britain today?

- Ask pupils to create a 'time capsule' — either real, drawn or written — that represents how they think their society should be remembered. Why have they included what they have? Does their record differ from the news clip? If so, how and why?

- Split pupils into groups and show them some everyday items, such as scissors and forks. Ask them to imagine they don't know what the objects are. Using only what they can see, get each group to present a different use for the objects to the rest of the class. E.g. a fork has pointed prongs, suggesting it could be used as a comb or a back-scratcher. Ask pupils to consider whether it's always possible to correctly work out an object's function simply by looking at it. How might this lead to different interpretations of prehistoric evidence?

Discover & Learn British History — Stone Age to Celts

How We Discover Prehistory

Study Book (pages 4-5)

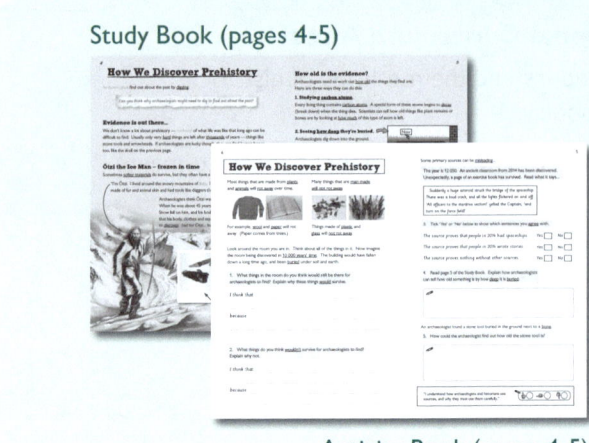

Activity Book (pages 4-5)

National Curriculum Aims
- Understand the methods of historical enquiry.
- Understand how evidence is used to make historical claims.
- Understand why there are different interpretations of the past.

Introduction

This topic allows pupils to learn about the archaeological methods used to research prehistory. To help pupils understand why the evidence available to archaeologists is limited, ask them to think of things they have seen begin to decay — e.g. food in a compost bin. The food begins to rot, but the plastic bin does not. Get the class to think about what items a future archaeologist would be able to discover from their lives. What would survive? What wouldn't? Would this give a full and accurate picture of their lives?

Answers to Activity Book Questions

1. E.g. *I think that* archaeologists would find my pen, my ruler, the trays, the chairs, the computer and my water bottle *because* they are made of man-made things like plastic and glass which don't rot away.
2. E.g. *I think that* my books, our paintings, my jumper, my scarf and the posters on the wall wouldn't survive *because* they all come from plants or animals, so they will rot away.
3. No — No — Yes
4. The deeper something is buried in the ground, the older it is.
5. E.g. The archaeologist could use carbon dating to work out how old the bone is. The stone tool was buried next to it, so it'll be about the same age.

Extra Activities

- Ötzi the Ice Man was an incredible find because he was so well preserved. Ötzi is now on display at a museum in Italy. In groups, get pupils to use the internet to research different aspects of Ötzi's discovery — where was he found? Who found him? What did he have with him? How did he die? Pupils should share their research with the class and then produce a leaflet for visitors to the museum describing Ötzi and his discovery.
- Create an archaeological site by burying some items in a sandpit, then ask pupils to find them as archaeologists would. Encourage them to think about how they should approach the task — why is it important to dig very carefully? What tools could they use? Would a paintbrush be useful?
- Ask pupils to imagine they are archaeologists about to start on a new prehistoric dig. Ask them to write a diary entry about the project — what are they going to take with them? What do they hope to find? How do they feel?

The First People in Britain

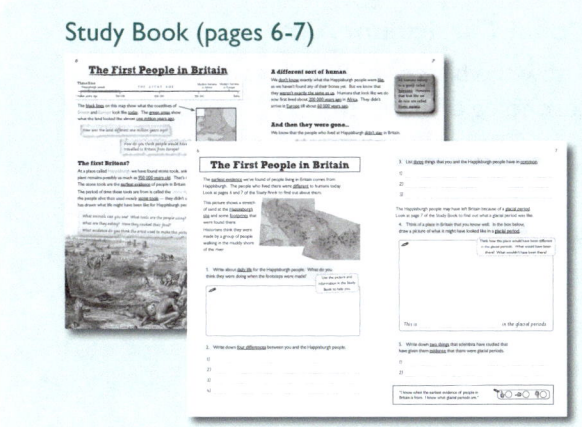

Study Book (pages 6-7)

Activity Book (pages 6-7)

National Curriculum Aims
- Know the history of Britain as a chronological narrative.
- Understand similarity and difference and use them to draw contrasts.
- Create structured accounts.

Introduction

Happisburgh, on the Norfolk coast, is a site of great significance in British history and in world prehistory. The footprints found there are the earliest known human footprints outside of Africa. Archaeologists have also found a vast number of tools at several different depths underground, indicating that there was a sustained human presence in the area. However, the site presents many challenges for archaeologists. It's much too old for carbon dating, which can only be used to date sites that are less than about 50 000 years old. Instead, archaeologists have dated the site by looking at the rocks beneath the earth's surface and evidence from the remains of plants and animals. By piecing together the footprints and artefacts at Happisburgh, we can begin to understand the lifestyle and physical appearance of the first people in Britain.

Answers to Activity Book Questions

1. E.g. Gathering plants that they could eat. / Hunting animals using stone and wooden tools. / Washing in the river. / Eating food by the river.

2. E.g. The Happisburgh people had to hunt for their own food. / They didn't wear clothes. / They didn't cook their food. / They didn't live in houses. / They lived alongside wild animals.

3. E.g. The Happisburgh people lived with other people. / They had to eat to stay alive. / They walked on two legs. / They used tools. / They ate meat. / They had families.

4. Pupils should show that it would be cold, e.g. by drawing ice or glaciers. They should recognise that there wouldn't be any modern landmarks such as buildings, and may have included suggestions of what would have been there instead.

5. ice cores / cores from the sea bed / the remains of organisms in sea bed cores

Extra Activities

- As a class, discuss pupils' answers to questions 2 and 3 in the Activity Book. Encourage pupils to look beyond material differences and similarities. Would Happisburgh children have had any of the same dreams or fears? What games might they have played? What might they have argued with their siblings about?

- Split the class into pairs and ask each pair to write an interview between a modern journalist and a member of the Happisburgh people. Questions could cover day-to-day activities, as well as how the Happisburgh people felt about various aspects of their lives. Ask volunteers to perform their interviews for the class.

- The Happisburgh people are thought to have left Britain because the climate became colder. Ask pupils to think about what their own ideal climate would be. What would the weather be like? What plants and animals would survive in that climate? Why would pupils be well suited to that climate?

Early Humans in Britain

Study Book (pages 8-9)

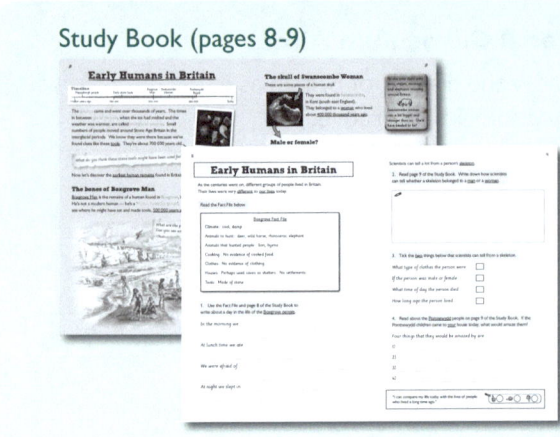

Activity Book (pages 8-9)

National Curriculum Aims
- Know the history of Britain as a chronological narrative.
- Create structured accounts.
- Understand the methods of historical enquiry.
- Understand how evidence is used to make historical claims.

Introduction

In this topic, pupils will learn about the earliest human remains found in Britain and what they can tell us about life in the early Stone Age. Once pupils have read pages 8-9 in the Study Book, discuss with them what a day in the life of an early human in Britain might have been like. Remind pupils that there would have been no money or shops, so people would have had to find everything they needed themselves. Ask pupils to consider what skills people would have needed to survive in early Stone Age Britain. Do pupils think that they have the necessary skills? You could then ask pupils to come up with words they would use to describe life in the early Stone Age. These words may be quite negative (e.g. difficult, scary, dangerous), but encourage pupils to think about the positive aspects of Stone Age life too. What modern dangers would not have existed? There were no wars or guns, the air was clean and there was no traffic. There was probably very little fighting over resources, as there were abundant sources of food and a very small population.

Answers to Activity Book Questions

1. Pupils' sentences should draw on the information given in the Fact File and on page 8 in the Study Book.
2. Some bones are different in men and women. For example, a man's skull is different from a woman's skull, and women have a wider pelvis.
3. Pupils should have ticked: If the person was male or female. AND How long ago the person lived.
4. E.g. television / radio / oven / the stairs / windows / the fridge / the freezer / the washing machine / all of the food in the house / the central heating / that we have our own bedrooms

Extra Activities

- The excavation site at Boxgrove is a Site of Special Scientific Interest and is also protected by English Heritage. Ask pupils to imagine that an archaeologist has said that the site doesn't deserve to be protected in this way. Using the internet, pupils could research the site and its significance, then write a speech explaining why preserving the site is important.

- Ask pupils to draw a picture of what they think life was like in early Stone Age Britain, then get them to share their drawings with the rest of the class. Discuss whether the drawings accurately represent the period. Why or why not?

- Lions, rhinos, monkeys and elephants were all found in early Stone Age Britain. Ask pupils how they would feel about living alongside these animals. Would it be scary? Would it be interesting? Get pupils to write a story exploring what life would be like if these animals still lived in Britain today.

Life in the Glacial Periods

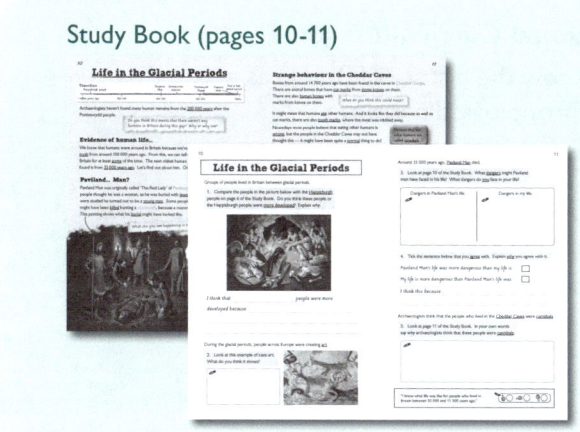

Study Book (pages 10-11)

Activity Book (pages 10-11)

National Curriculum Aims
- Know the history of Britain as a chronological narrative.
- Understand similarity and difference and use them to draw contrasts.
- Understand change.
- Understand how evidence is used to make historical claims.

Introduction

We have very little evidence about life in Britain during the early Stone Age, and the pieces of evidence that do survive originated many thousands of years apart. Despite their scarcity, these pieces of evidence offer important — and sometimes surprising — insights into the behaviour of Stone Age Britons. For example, the human tooth marks found on human bones in Cheddar Gorge suggest that some Stone Age Britons may have practised cannibalism. As a class, discuss why we may be disgusted by Stone Age behaviours like cannibalism. Ask pupils to consider whether it is because there is something fundamentally wrong with such behaviours, or if it is simply that they are unfamiliar to us? What might Stone Age people find disgusting about us?

Answers to Activity Book Questions

1. *I think that* these *people were more developed*.
   E.g. They've learned how to make fire. This means they can cook food and keep themselves warm.

2. a group of deer / stags

3. E.g. *Dangers in Paviland Man's life*: getting hurt hunting animals / wild animals getting into his cave / not finding enough food
   Dangers in my life: cars on busy roads / sharp objects / hot objects / fireworks / getting lost

4. Pupils may answer either way, as long as they give a sensible reason to support their answer.

5. E.g. They found human bones that had marks made by stone knives and teeth on them. This made them think that people had eaten the meat off the bones.

Extra Activities

- As a class, make a list of the uses of fire (e.g. light, warmth, protection, cooking) and discuss the significance of humans learning to make fire. Ask pupils to identify other discoveries that have brought about major changes in the way humans live. Get them to pick the three they think have had the biggest impact and explain their reasoning.

- Challenge pupils to find Cheddar Gorge on a map. Then ask pupils to draw a map of Britain with Cheddar Gorge labelled on it, as well as other places mentioned so far in the Study Book where evidence of early Stone Age Britons has been found (e.g. Happisburgh, Boxgrove, Swanscombe, Pontnewydd, Paviland Cave in south Wales). Ask for volunteers to explain why each place is historically significant.

- Ask pupils to imagine that they can only communicate through a series of very simple pictures or 'drawings on cave walls'. Get them to create their own cave drawing depicting what they did at the weekend.

The Mesolithic

Study Book (pages 12-13)

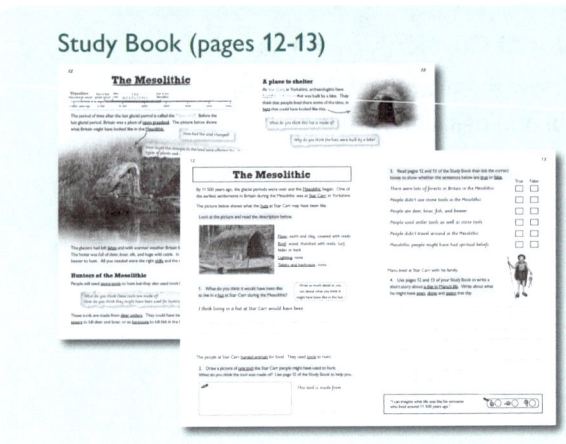

Activity Book (pages 12-13)

National Curriculum Aims

- Know the history of Britain as a chronological narrative.
- Create structured accounts.
- Understand how evidence is used to make historical claims.

Introduction

The Mesolithic period, which began when the last glacial period ended, saw significant innovation and progress as Mesolithic communities adapted to changes in their environment. The warmer climate brought new animals to Britain, causing Mesolithic people to develop new hunting tools and techniques, and to change their diet. There were also social changes. At Star Carr, archaeologists have found evidence of sophisticated permanent structures. This suggests that, unlike their predecessors, Mesolithic people were not completely nomadic, but occupied some sites on a seasonal basis. Once pupils have read pages 12-13 in the Study Book, discuss the advantages and disadvantages of building settlements compared to living an exclusively nomadic lifestyle.

Answers to Activity Book Questions

1. Pupils should draw on the information given to produce a detailed description. E.g. They could infer that it would have been cold / uncomfortable / dark.

2. Pupils could draw a spear or harpoon (as on page 12 in the Study Book) or a stone tool.
   This tool is made from deer antler / stone.

3. True — False — True — True — False — True

4. Pupils' stories should be based on information from the Study Book. As well as including details about Manu's daily life (e.g. hunting, his hut, spiritual beliefs), encourage them to describe how they think Manu might have felt.

Extra Activities

- Pupils could consider what skills are important at school (e.g. reading, writing and maths), and whether the same skills were important for people at Star Carr. Ask pupils to write a list of skills that they think would have helped them to survive in Mesolithic Britain.

- As a class, discuss materials that would have been available during the Mesolithic period. Which materials would be good for building a hut? Which would be waterproof or provide shelter? Which would be most practical? Pupils could write down the pros and cons of different materials and then build a scale model of a Mesolithic hut using the materials they have identified as being most suitable.

- Remind pupils that our opinions about aspects of Mesolithic life may be very different from the opinions of people alive at the time. For example, to Manu, the hut at Star Carr may have represented warmth, safety and shelter. Carry out a hot-seating exercise, with one pupil taking on the role of Manu and another answering as themselves. The rest of the class should ask them questions about their attitudes towards various aspects of life in the Mesolithic period.

Life in the Mesolithic

Study Book (pages 14-15)

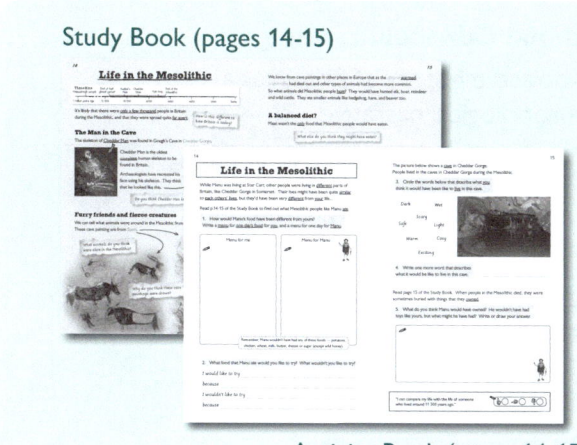

Activity Book (pages 14-15)

National Curriculum Aims

- Know the history of Britain as a chronological narrative.

- Understand similarity and difference and use them to draw contrasts.

Introduction

This topic gives pupils an insight into the similarities and differences between their lives and life in the Mesolithic. It also encourages them to challenge their perceptions of the past. Before pupils read pages 14-15 in the Study Book, make sure they understand the term 'hunter-gatherer' and ask them whether they think that Mesolithic people's diets were more or less varied than their own. Explain that thanks to the hunter-gatherer lifestyle, the Mesolithic diet was in many ways more varied than ours. A large part of our diet now comes from wheat, rice and potatoes, but people in the Mesolithic period ate a wide range of meats, seafood and plants. Archaeologists have found trout and salmon bones at Mesolithic sites, as well as shells from periwinkles and limpets. Far from being limited, the Mesolithic diet even featured frogs' legs and a sort of chewing gum made from birch bark tar!

Answers to Activity Book Questions

1. E.g. *Menu for me*: pupils should give a list of foods they eat.
   Menu for Manu: fish / hare / boar / beaver / wild cattle / hedgehog / elk / reindeer / some vegetables

2. Any appropriate answer.

3. Any appropriate answer.

4. The word written here should tie in with the words chosen above.

5. E.g. weapons / a head dress / jewellery / clothes

Extra Activities

- Explain to the class that hunter-gatherers' diets would change throughout the year depending on what was in season. Ask pupils to research which fruits and vegetables are in season in modern Britain in the spring, summer, autumn and winter, and then produce a poster to display their findings. As a class, discuss how pupils' diets would change if they only ate locally-sourced, seasonal produce.

- In pairs, get pupils to discuss whether they would rather live in a Mesolithic hut or in a cave. Then ask pupils to write a story about meeting someone who lives in a cave. How do they meet them? What is the person like? Why are they living in a cave? What is their day-to-day life like?

- Ask pupils to think about what Manu might have valued most. Ask them to imagine Manu going on a journey where he could only take a few things with him. What would he take? Ask pupils to think about what they value. If they could take only ten things on a long journey, what would they take and why?

Discover & Learn British History — Stone Age to Celts

Changes in the Mesolithic

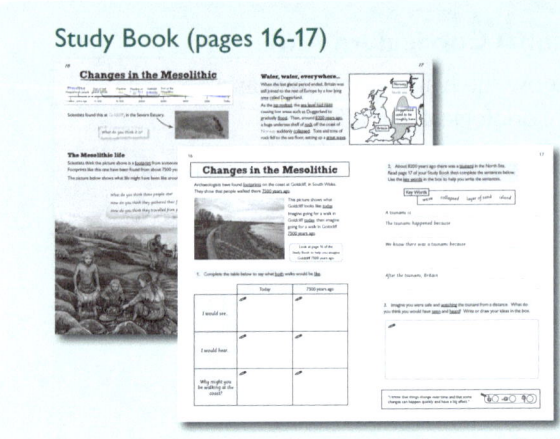

Study Book (pages 16-17)

Activity Book (pages 16-17)

National Curriculum Aims
- Know the history of Britain as a chronological narrative.
- Understand cause and consequence.
- Understand continuity, change and significance.
- Understand similarity and difference and use them to draw contrasts.

Introduction

Britain was once connected to the rest of Europe by a vast area of land called Doggerland, which was home to thousands of people. In the Mesolithic period, a huge tsunami flooded Doggerland, causing Britain to become an island. Today, Doggerland is a site of great archaeological interest. Sets of human footprints have been found on the sea floor, along with mammoth bones and hunting artefacts. Researchers working with oil companies have recently been able to look at the area in more detail to build up a picture of what the landscape used to be like. Using sophisticated technology, they have found evidence of coastlines, hills, lakes and rivers. It is hoped that further research will uncover more about Doggerland's environment and the people who lived there.

Answers to Activity Book Questions

1. E.g. *Today I would see* joggers.   *7500 years ago I would see* huts.
   Today I would hear cars.   *7500 years ago I would hear* birds.
   Today I might be walking for exercise.   *7500 years ago* I might have been walking to find food.

2. *A tsunami is* a great wave.
   The tsunami happened because a huge undersea shelf of rock off the coast of Norway suddenly collapsed.
   We know there was a tsunami because a layer of sand was found in between layers of peat, 50 miles inland and 4 metres above the normal tide line in Scotland.
   After the tsunami, Britain became an island.

3. Pupils should show they understand that the tsunami was a great wave which came a long way inland.

Extra Activities

- As a class, discuss the significance of the tsunami in the history of Britain. How might life be different if Britain was still joined to the rest of Europe today?
- Ask pupils to write a newspaper article telling the story of a fisherman who has found mammoth bones at Dogger Bank, an area of Doggerland situated around 80 miles off the Yorkshire coast. Encourage them to think about how the discovery happened and what it might mean for future research at the site.
- As a class, discuss how the landscape of the local area has changed over time. Ask pupils to do some research and find old maps and pictures of their area or town. What changes can pupils see? Are they natural or man-made? Why do they think these changes took place?

The Neolithic

Study Book (pages 18-19)

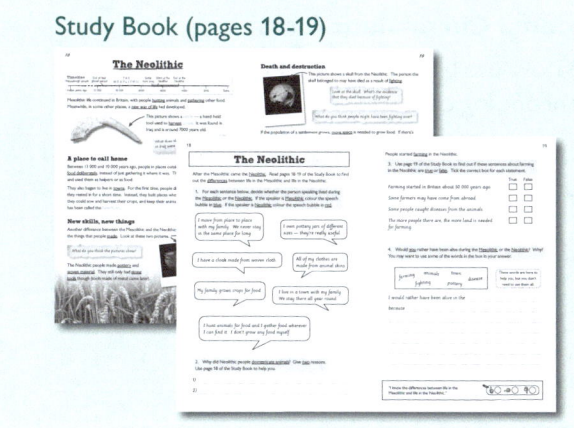

Activity Book (pages 18-19)

National Curriculum Aims

- Know the history of Britain as a chronological narrative.
- Understand similarity and difference and use them to draw contrasts.
- Understand continuity and change.

Introduction

The Neolithic period is the era when agriculture is thought to have been introduced to Britain from Europe. Before the Neolithic period, most communities were completely or semi-nomadic, but with the advent of farming permanent settlements developed. Archaeologists aren't sure why people in Britain abandoned their hunter-gatherer lifestyle and adopted agriculture. Farming meant preparing and maintaining land, which arguably involved more work than hunting and gathering. An agricultural lifestyle may also have given people less food security — a static population could face famine if crops failed, whereas nomadic groups could move on and search for food elsewhere. Ask pupils why they think people might have wanted to become farmers.

Answers to Activity Book Questions

1. Pupils should have coloured the following sentences blue:
   I move from place to place with my family. We never stay in the same place for long.
   All of my clothes are made from animal skins.
   I hunt animals for food and I gather food wherever I can find it. I don't grow any food myself.
   The other sentences should be coloured red.

2. To use them as helpers. / To use them as food.

3. False — True — True — True

4. Pupils may answer either way, as long as they give sensible reasons to support their answer.

Extra Activities

- Ask pupils to make a list of modern domesticated animals (e.g. cows, chickens, horses, dogs) and write down what each animal can be used for. Which animal do they think would have been the most useful to a Neolithic community?

- Using modelling clay, ask pupils to make their own Neolithic pot based on the picture on page 18 in the Study Book. Encourage them to try and replicate the shape of the pot, as well as its decoration.

- Split pupils into small groups and assign half the groups the Mesolithic and half the Neolithic. Ask each group to come up with a short play showing what daily life was like in their assigned period. After pupils have performed their plays, discuss the differences between daily life in the two periods.

- Using their answers to question 4 in the Activity Book and the ideas discussed in the previous activity, ask pupils to create a poster that would convince someone from the Mesolithic to adopt a Neolithic lifestyle or vice versa. Encourage them to use persuasive language and to illustrate their poster.

Discover & Learn British History — Stone Age to Celts

Neolithic Village Life

Study Book (pages 20-21)

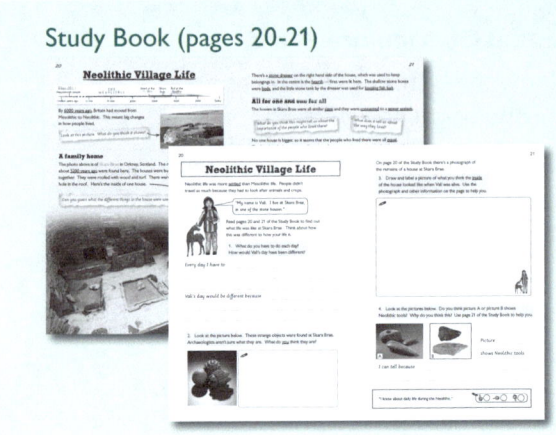

Activity Book (pages 20-21)

National Curriculum Aims

- Know the history of Britain as a chronological narrative.
- Understand similarity and difference and use them to draw contrasts.
- Understand how evidence is used to make historical claims.
- Understand why there are different interpretations of the past.

Introduction

Skara Brae was discovered by chance. When a storm hit Orkney in 1850, the wind and high tides stripped the grass from a mound which had been known as 'Skerrabra'. This uncovered the outline of some stone buildings. Amateur excavation began, but Skara Brae wasn't seriously excavated until the 1920s. Because it was protected from the elements for over 4000 years, the site is remarkably well preserved. Studying it gives pupils the chance to explore an outstanding and hugely useful collection of evidence from the Neolithic period. Once pupils have read pages 20-21 in the Study Book, show them some more pictures of Skara Brae and discuss the different things they can see.

Answers to Activity Book Questions

1. Pupils should make the differences between their day and Vali's day clear.

2. Any appropriate answer. There is debate over whether the objects were used as weapons, carried as symbols of power or were even works of art. Pupils should think about what they look like, whether they remind them of anything and how they could have been used.

3. Pupils' drawings should show a house made from flat rocks. The roof should be made of turf and wood and have a smoke hole. There shouldn't be any windows. Pupils may have included details such as a central hearth, a stone dresser, beds and a tank for fish bait.

4. *Picture A shows Neolithic tools.*
   E.g. *I can tell because* the tools look smooth and people in the Neolithic ground and polished their tools.

Extra Activities

- Ask pupils to imagine being the person who first discovered the ruins at Skara Brae. Get them to write a letter to a friend telling them all about it. What did they think when they first saw the ruins? Did they realise the significance of what they had found? How did they feel?

- Explain to pupils that the organisations responsible for the conservation of Skara Brae face a number of challenges. The site is visited by a large number of tourists every year, and it is also sandy, coastal and hit by frequent storms. As a class, discuss why each of these factors might pose a threat to the site. Can pupils think of any measures that could be taken to help preserve Skara Brae?

- Show pupils more pictures of Neolithic tools from the internet. Ask them to choose one of the tools and make a model of it. As a class, discuss the similarities and differences between Neolithic tools and the tools we use today. Do pupils think Neolithic tools would have been more or less effective than our tools?

Discover & Learn British History — Stone Age to Celts

Neolithic Stone Circles

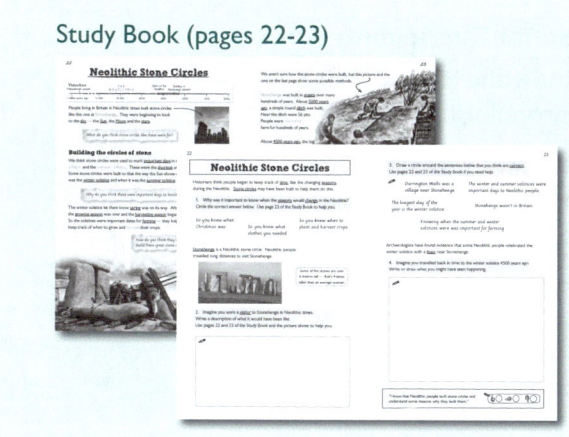

Study Book (pages 22-23)

Activity Book (pages 22-23)

National Curriculum Aims
- Know the history of Britain as a chronological narrative.
- Create structured accounts.
- Understand how evidence is used to make historical claims.

Introduction

Today, over 1000 stone circles can be found dotted around the British Isles. It cannot be known for certain why they were built, but many different theories have been put forward. One widespread theory is that they were used to track the movement of the sun — by arranging the stones in a particular way, Neolithic people could try to make sense of the sun's cycles. For example, it has been observed that Stonehenge, the best-known stone circle in Britain, is aligned with the direction of sunrise on the summer solstice. Some of Stonehenge's stones weigh as much as 25 tons, so it is likely that hundreds of people would have been needed to move and erect them. The amount of effort involved in constructing this huge stone circle, and others around the country, demonstrates how important they were to Neolithic people.

Answers to Activity Book Questions

1. Pupils should have circled: So you knew when to plant and harvest crops.
2. Any appropriate answer. Pupils should think about how big the stones are, how they're arranged and what they would have thought of them.
3. Pupils should have circled:
   Durrington Walls was a village near Stonehenge.
   The winter and summer solstices were important days to Neolithic people.
   Knowing when the summer and winter solstices were was important for farming.
4. Any appropriate answer. Encourage pupils to use their imaginations. E.g. What might the weather have been like? What would people have been wearing? What would they have been eating?

Extra Activities

- Ask pupils to find pictures on the internet of how Stonehenge looks today, and then ask them to research the size of the stones that are still standing. Get pupils to use the pictures and information they have found to make a scale model of Stonehenge as it looks now. As a class, put together a list of the challenges the people building Stonehenge would have faced. How might they have overcome these challenges?
- The stones at Stonehenge may have been transported on rollers. Pupils could model this using books or bricks to represent the stones, and pencils as rollers. Ask pupils to think about how the stones might be moved today. What technology do we now have that would make the task easier?
- Stonehenge is now a popular tourist attraction. Using books and the internet, ask pupils to find further information about Stonehenge. Pupils could then make a poster advertising Stonehenge.

Discover & Learn British History — Stone Age to Celts

Flint, Copper and Bronze

Study Book (pages 24-25)

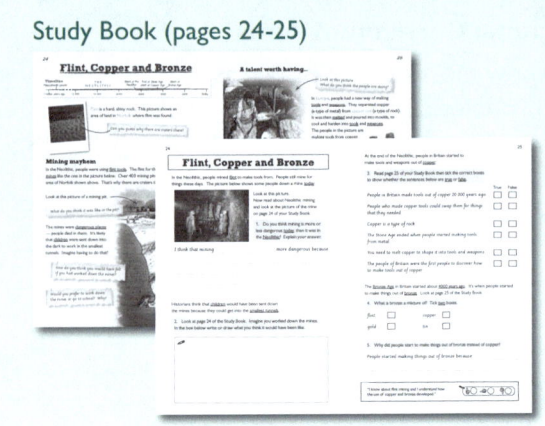

Activity Book (pages 24-25)

National Curriculum Aims

- Know the history of Britain as a chronological narrative.
- Know how people's lives have shaped Britain.
- Understand similarity and difference and use them to draw contrasts.

Introduction

Between c.2500 BC and c.2000 BC, the Stone Age gradually came to an end in Britain as people began to use metal tools instead of stone ones. Initially, it was copper that replaced stone, but bronze (a stronger, harder metal, made from a mixture of copper and tin) gained popularity relatively quickly. This shift to copper and bronze was facilitated by the availability of vast resources of copper and tin, especially in south-west England and north Wales. By studying the transition from stone to copper and bronze, pupils can track technological progress in prehistoric times and see how materials were selected and improved upon based on society's needs. Once pupils have read pages 24-25 in the Study Book, ask the class what Neolithic people used flint for and write a list on the board. Why do pupils think copper and bronze might have been better materials to use?

Answers to Activity Book Questions

1. *I think that mining* in the Neolithic was *more dangerous*.
   Pupils might comment on differences in safety standards and equipment between the Neolithic and now.

2. Any appropriate answer. Pupils should think about how they would have felt. Would it have been cold? Would there be much light? Would you have felt scared? Why?

3. False — True — False — True — True — False

4. Pupils should have ticked: copper AND tin.

5. *People started making things out of bronze because* it was harder and stronger than copper.

Extra Activities

- Split the class into groups and ask each group to research either flint, copper or bronze. Ask them to find out whether we still use each material today, what it's used for, how we extract/make it, what its properties are and to find some pictures of it. Each group should then produce a fact file on their material.

- Ask pupils to imagine they have just arrived in Stone Age Britain from Europe, bringing some copper with them. Ask them to create an advert that will persuade people to replace their flint tools with copper ones. Encourage them to think about the aesthetic appeal of the metal as well as its physical properties.

- Explain to the class that lots of different materials have been mined in different parts of Britain through the centuries and that some mines are still working today. Split the class into groups and assign each group a region of the UK (e.g. Wales, Scotland, Devon and Cornwall, Lancashire, Yorkshire). Ask each group to research what is/was mined in their assigned area, what the mined material can be used for and whether any mines are still operating today.

Life After the Stone Age

Study Book (pages 26-27)

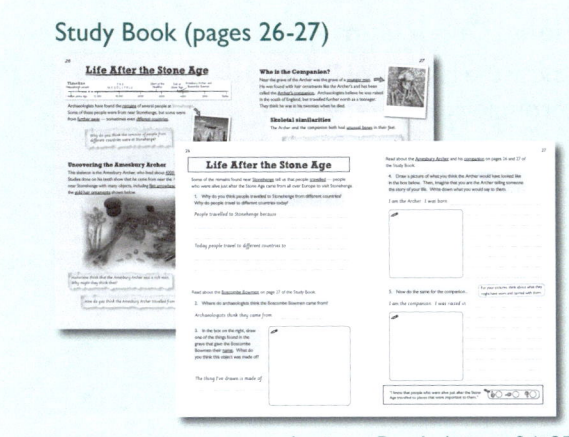

Activity Book (pages 26-27)

National Curriculum Aims
- Know the history of Britain as a chronological narrative.
- Create structured accounts.
- Understand how evidence is used to make historical claims.

Introduction

By studying prehistoric travellers like the Amesbury Archer and the Boscombe Bowmen, pupils can gain a greater understanding of post-Stone Age society and culture. Ask pupils to think back to when they studied Stonehenge — can they remember any of the theories about why people travelled there and why the site was important? Once pupils have read pages 26-27 in the Study Book, show them a map of Europe and point out the location of the Alps and Stonehenge. Ask pupils what they think the journey from the Alps to Stonehenge would have been like in prehistoric times. What challenges would the journey have involved? E.g. trekking through mountains, travelling across Europe, crossing the Channel. Are pupils surprised that people were willing to undertake such a difficult and potentially dangerous journey to reach Stonehenge?

Answers to Activity Book Questions

1. E.g. *People travelled to Stonehenge because* they thought it was an important place / they wanted to celebrate the summer and winter solstices.
   Today people travel to different countries to go on holiday / visit their families.
2. *Archaeologists think they came from* Wales.
3. Pupils should have drawn an arrowhead. *The thing I've drawn is made of:* flint / bone.
4. Any appropriate answer. Pupils should draw on information from the Study Book.
5. Any appropriate answer. Pupils should draw on information from the Study Book.

Extra Activities

- Make a list on the board of pupils' answers to question 1 in the Activity Book. How many different reasons did the class come up with for why people travelled to Stonehenge and why people travel abroad today? As a class, discuss the similarities and differences between the reasons why people travel now and why they travelled in prehistoric times.

- Ask pupils to write an account of the longest journey they can remember taking. How did they travel? How much did they see or notice on their journey? Did they interact with people on the way? Then ask them to imagine doing the same journey on foot. How would their experience have been different?

- Discuss with pupils the items that were found buried with the Amesbury Archer and the Boscombe Bowmen. Why do pupils think they were buried with these items? What do these items tell us about the Archer and the Bowmen? Get pupils to draw items they think people might want to be buried with today and then discuss their drawings as class. How are these items similar or different to those buried with prehistoric people?

Discover & Learn British History — Stone Age to Celts

Bronze Age Travel and Trade

Study Book (pages 28-29)

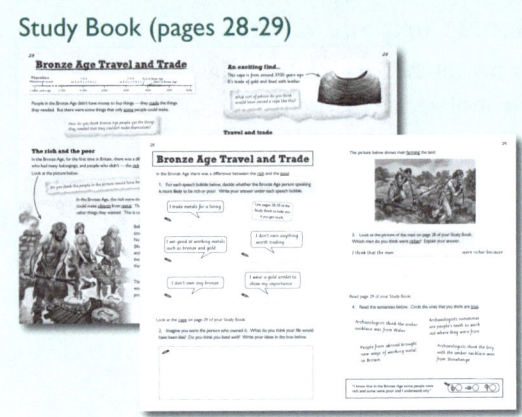

Activity Book (pages 28-29)

National Curriculum Aims

- Know the history of Britain as a chronological narrative.
- Understand similarity and difference and use them to draw contrasts.
- Understand how evidence is used to make historical claims.

Introduction

Many of the social and economic changes which occurred in the Bronze Age are still recognisable in our society today. Clear distinctions between rich and poor first began to emerge in Britain in the Bronze Age. Rich people owned, worked and traded metal, which gave them status in their communities. It also enabled them to trade with visitors to Britain from elsewhere. This created connections between Britain and places like northern France, Scandinavia and even the Mediterranean, and facilitated the sharing of ideas, knowledge and culture as well as material goods. Make sure pupils understand that social structures based on wealth, long-distance trade and the import and export of goods are still part of life in modern Britain.

Answers to Activity Book Questions

1. Pupils should have written poor underneath the following sentences:
   I don't own anything worth trading.
   I don't own any bronze.
   Pupils should have written rich underneath the other sentences.

2. Pupils should think about what the cape is made of and what clues that gives us.

3. *I think that the men* working the metal *were richer*.
   E.g. Because they would have been able to make things that they could trade.

4. Pupils should have circled:
   Archaeologists sometimes use people's teeth to work out where they were from.
   People from abroad brought new ways of working metal to Britain.

Extra Activities

- As a class, discuss how modern travel and trade links compare to those in the Bronze Age. Would people in the Bronze Age have been able to travel as widely as we can? Would they have been able to buy things from as many different parts of the world?

- Explain to pupils that the gold cape shown on page 29 in the Study Book is called the Mold Cape and was discovered in 1833 by some men working in a quarry in Mold, north Wales. Ask pupils to design their own Bronze Age cape, based on the Mold Cape. Encourage them to think about the shape of the cape and the decoration on it, as well as the materials they would have had access to in the Bronze Age.

- Ask pupils whether they think our society is equal. Is it possible to have a society where everyone has the same amount of money and belongings? Do pupils think this would be more or less fair than our society? You could hold a debate on this topic, with half the class arguing in favour of a more equal distribution of wealth and the other half arguing against it.

Life in the Bronze Age

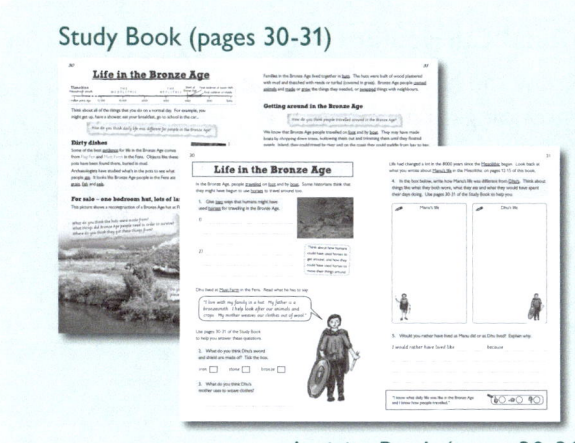

Study Book (pages 30-31)

Activity Book (pages 30-31)

National Curriculum Aims

- Know the history of Britain as a chronological narrative.
- Understand similarity and difference and use them to draw contrasts.
- Understand change.

Introduction

This topic explores several different aspects of everyday life in the Bronze Age, allowing pupils to see the progress that occurred during this era and to draw comparisons with earlier periods of prehistory. Get pupils to think about how we can measure progress. What kinds of things can we compare? Discuss technological change, changes in social structures, changes in lifestyles, etc. Ask pupils whether they think that all change is progress. Do they think that progress is necessarily always a good thing? Encourage the class to think about whether progress is still being made today. Can they think of any examples of progress in modern society?

Answers to Activity Book Questions

1. E.g. They could have ridden horses to travel about. / They could have had carts pulled by horses to carry their belongings around in.
2. Pupils should have ticked: bronze.
3. a loom
4. E.g. *Manu's life*: tools and weapons made of stone and antler / hunted and gathered food / ate fish, boar, elk and vegetables / no woven clothes
   Dhu's life: weapons made of bronze / farmed crops / kept animals / ate grains, fish and eel / woven clothes
5. Pupils may answer either way, as long as they give sensible reasons to support their answer. They may use their answer to question 4 to help explain their opinion.

Extra Activities

- Pupils could make simple cardboard 'looms' and use them to weave their own cloth. They should start by cutting small, evenly-spaced slits into the shorter edges of an A6-size piece of card, and looping a piece of wool vertically around the card, with one loop in each slit. They can then weave a different-coloured piece of wool horizontally over and under the loops.

- Get pupils to look at the huts described on pages 30-31 in the Study Book, and then look back at the huts from Star Carr and Skara Brae (pages 13 and 20 in the Study Book). Ask pupils to produce a short piece of writing comparing the different structures. Can pupils see how the huts have developed? What different materials have begun to be used? Are there any similarities?

- As a class, discuss how pupils' lives now compare with the lives of children like Dhu in the Bronze Age. Which features of Dhu's life are still part of life today? E.g. woven clothes / travel on foot, by boat and perhaps using wheeled vehicles / farmed crops / domesticated animals.

Discover & Learn British History — Stone Age to Celts

The End of the Bronze Age

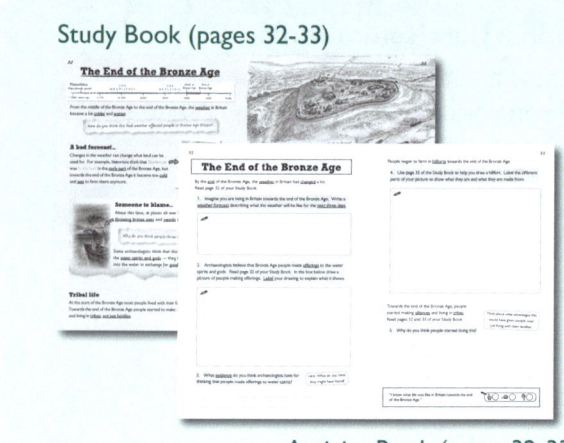

Study Book (pages 32-33)

Activity Book (pages 32-33)

National Curriculum Aims
- Know the history of Britain as a chronological narrative.
- Understand cause and consequence.
- Understand how evidence is used to make historical claims.
- Understand change.

Introduction

Towards the end of the Bronze Age, Britain changed in some significant ways, and so did the lifestyle of the people living there. The climate became colder and wetter, which made life much more difficult. For example the risk of flooding increased, making some areas of farmland uncultivable. At the same time, people began to live with defence in mind, moving away from small, largely family-based groups and instead forming larger tribes, some of which constructed hillforts. Living in a tribe gave people greater support and security, and hillforts provided good protection thanks to their elevated positions and walled perimeters. Once pupils have read pages 32-33 in the Study Book, ask them to think about why people in the late Bronze Age might have become more concerned with war and protection. Why do pupils think there was more violence than in earlier times?

Answers to Activity Book Questions

1. Pupils should show that the weather was cold and wet.
2. Pupils' drawings should show Bronze Age people throwing metal goods such as swords, shields and axes into a river or stream.
3. E.g. I think they might have found weapons like bronze swords and axes in rivers and streams.
4. Pupils' drawings should show a fort on top of a hill. The top of the hill should be surrounded by a wall made of earth, wood or stone. There should be buildings and farming taking place within the hillfort. The different features of the hillfort should be labelled.
5. E.g. I think people started making alliances and living in tribes because if you lived in a tribe there were more people to protect you and defend your land if you were attacked.

Extra Activities

- Pupils have learnt that there was a change in climate at the end of the Bronze Age. Ask them to think about what living in a hut would have been like when the climate became colder and wetter, then write a diary entry about it. How might the weather have made them feel? How would it have affected daily life?

- As a class, discuss pupils' answers to question 5 in the Activity Book and make a list of the advantages and disadvantages of being part of a larger tribe. Then, discuss similar social structures that exist today. What groups are pupils part of (e.g. school, sports clubs, country)? What do people in these groups share? What benefits come from being part of a group?

- Ask pupils to research and produce a slideshow on the late Bronze Age / early Iron Age hill fort at Mam Tor in the Peak District. Where is it? What defensive features did it have? What artefacts have been found there? What can be seen there today? Pupils should present their slideshow to the class.

The Celtic Age of Iron

Study Book (pages 34-35)

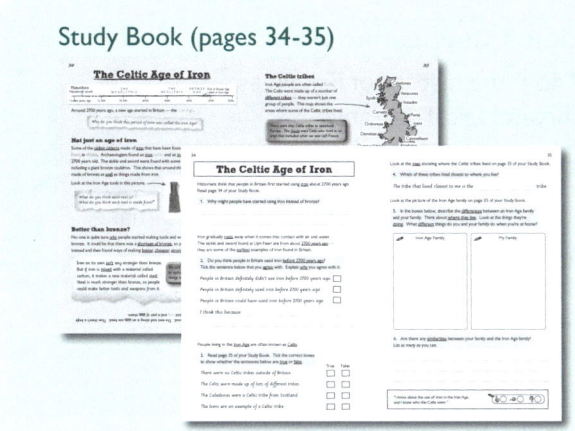

Activity Book (pages 34-35)

National Curriculum Aims

- Know the history of Britain as a chronological narrative.
- Understand cause and consequence.
- Understand how evidence is used to make historical claims.
- Understand similarity and difference and use them to draw contrasts.

Introduction

The introduction of iron-working technology to Britain from around 800 BC brought about major changes in British society and culture. More efficient iron-tipped farming equipment led to increased productivity and the ability to grow new crops. These agricultural developments facilitated significant population growth — the British population may have hit one million during the Iron Age. Studying the Iron Age will give pupils another opportunity to explore the challenges of building up an accurate picture of prehistoric Britain from the surviving evidence. Before pupils read pages 34-35 in the Study Book, make sure they understand the concept of rusting — you could show them some pictures of objects rusting away over time. Ask pupils to think about why this process might make it problematic to collect evidence from the Iron Age.

Answers to Activity Book Questions

1. E.g. There was a shortage of bronze. / They might have found ways of making better, cheaper, stronger items from iron.

2. Pupils should have ticked: People in Britain could have used iron before 2700 years ago.
   E.g. *I think this because* there might have been iron, but it might not have been found yet, or it could have rusted away.

3. False — True — True — True

4. Pupils should use the map on page 35 in the Study Book to name the Celtic tribe that lived closest to them.

5. E.g. *Iron Age Family*: They live in a hut. / They all live in one room.
   My Family: I live in a house. / We have our own bedrooms.

6. E.g. The children look like they are helping prepare their food and I help my parents prepare our food.

Extra Activities

- Ask pupils to find out more about how iron is made. What are its properties? How is it turned into steel? What do we use it for today? Pupils should make a poster displaying their findings.

- Pupils can explore rusting with a simple experiment. Place different objects (e.g. a nail, a plastic block, a sugar cube) into separate jars of water. Ask pupils what they think will happen to each item. Leave them for a few days. Students should monitor any changes — what do they notice?

- Ask pupils to research the Iron Age tribe that lived closest to them. Where did they live? Were they known for anything in particular? Have archaeologists found any evidence of this tribe's settlements? If so, what were they like? Pupils should put together an informative leaflet about the tribe.

Life in the Iron Age

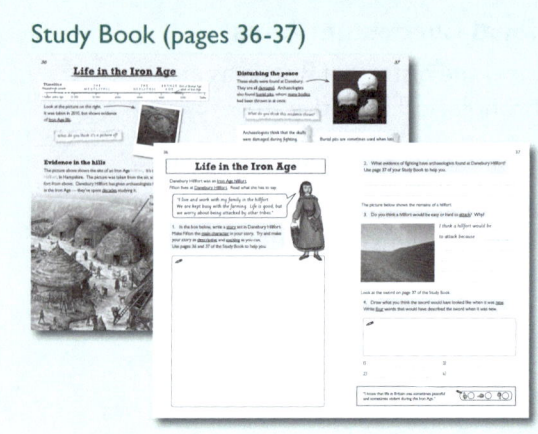

Study Book (pages 36-37)

Activity Book (pages 36-37)

National Curriculum Aims

- Know the history of Britain as a chronological narrative.
- Create structured accounts.
- Understand how evidence is used to make historical claims.

Introduction

One of the most significant social changes during the Iron Age was the emergence of large, independent tribes throughout Britain. A key way in which the leaders of these tribes won their followers' loyalty was by providing them with food security. The archaeological evidence suggests that relations between the British tribes could be quite turbulent and that fighting often took place. This is supported by written evidence from Roman visitors to Britain, who regarded Iron Age Britons as fierce, brave warriors. Despite their warlike reputation, Iron Age Britons were also skilled craftspeople. In addition to iron, they used materials like bronze, gold and coloured glass to produce intricately decorated objects such as shields and jewellery.

Answers to Activity Book Questions

1. Pupils' stories should draw on information from pages 36-37 in the Study Book. They might include some details about Fifion's daily life, an attack on the hillfort by another tribe and Fifion's reaction to the attack.
2. E.g. Archaeologists have found some damaged skulls and evidence of burial pits.
3. E.g. *I think a hillfort would be hard to attack because* the sides were steep, so they would be difficult to climb while carrying weapons and being attacked from above.
4. Any appropriate drawing and adjectives. E.g. shiny / sharp / heavy / dazzling

Extra Activities

- Ask pupils to draw a table with columns headed 'Mesolithic Age', 'Neolithic Age', 'Bronze Age' 'Iron Age', and rows headed 'housing', 'tools', 'food', 'clothes', 'travel'. Pupils should fill in their table with the information they have learnt from the Study Book. As a class, discuss the differences between the four periods. Then ask pupils to produce a short piece of writing identifying what they regard as the most significant difference between the Mesolithic Age and the Iron Age, and explaining their reasoning.

- People played many different roles in Iron Age society (e.g. leader, warrior, trader, craftsperson, druid). Split the class into groups and ask each group to research one of these roles. What was their function within the tribe? The class could make a wall display of a hillfort and present all the information that they have found within it.

- Ask pupils to look again at the sword handle pictured on page 37 in the Study Book, and show them images of some other Iron Age artefacts (e.g. the Wandsworth shield boss, the Battersea Shield, the Snettisham Great Torc). Ask pupils to design and make their own Iron Age accessory or shield. They could construct their artefact using papier-mâché and decorate it using tissue paper, foil, etc.

An Invasion from Rome

Study Book (pages 38-39)

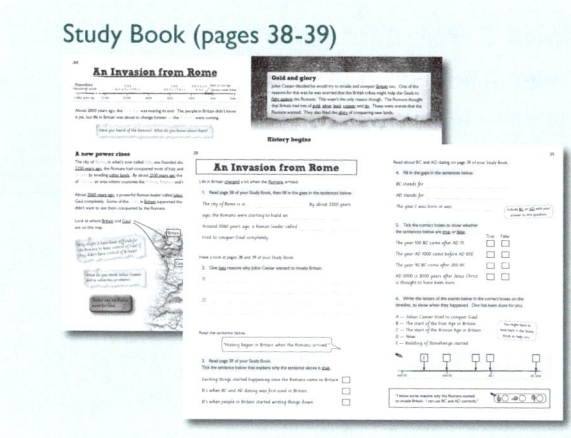

Activity Book (pages 38-39)

National Curriculum Aims

- Know the history of Britain as a chronological narrative.

- Know and understand significant aspects of the history of the wider world, for example, the expansion of empires.

- Know and use historical terms such as 'empire', 'AD' and 'BC'.

Introduction

At its height, the Roman Empire was one of the largest empires the world has ever known, encompassing much of Europe, as well as parts of Asia and North Africa. The arrival of the Romans in Britain led to major changes in British society and culture, and Roman influence is still felt today in everything from place names to styles of architecture. For historians, one of the most significant consequences of Roman contact with Britain was the introduction of literacy to the British Isles. Once pupils have read pages 38-39 in the Study Book, discuss why the spread of literacy is so significant. Why might written records be easier to interpret than archaeological sources? Can pupils think of any challenges historians might face when working with written sources?

Answers to Activity Book Questions

1. *The city of Rome is in* Italy. *By about 2250 years ago, the Romans were starting to build an* empire. *Around 2060 years ago, a Roman leader called* Julius Caesar *tried to conquer Gaul completely.*

2. E.g. To stop the tribes in Britain helping the people in Gaul fight the Romans. / To get metals such as gold, silver, lead, copper and tin. / For the glory of conquering new lands.

3. Pupils should have ticked: It's when people in Britain started writing things down.

4. *BC stands for* Before Christ.
   AD stands for Anno Domini.
   The year I was born in was: pupils should write AD and then the year they were born.

5. False — False — True — True

6. E — C — B — A — D

Extra Activities

- Give each pupil a card with a different year written on it (some BC, some AD). Ask pupils to line up in chronological order.

- Ask pupils to find out more about Julius Caesar. You could give them the following questions to help structure their research: When and where was he born? What roles did he play in the Roman Empire? When and how did he die? How do we know about him? Why is he important? Pupils should use their findings to write a short biography of Caesar. They may want to draw a picture of an event from his life to illustrate their work.

- As a class, create a timeline to illustrate the key developments in British prehistory. Split the class into groups and assign each group a period to cover — they should produce an illustrated summary of each notable development within their period. Combine everyone's work to make a whole class timeline.

Discover & Learn British History — Stone Age to Celts

The Romans Invade Britain

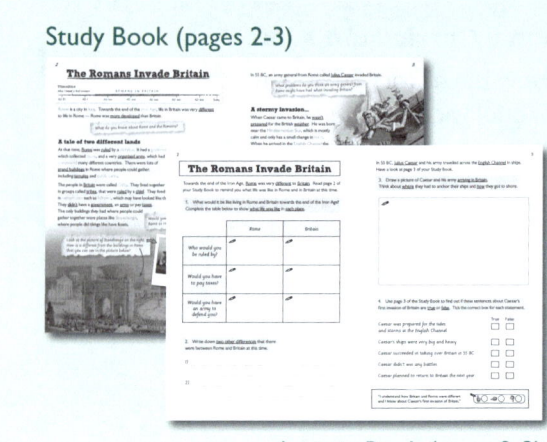

Study Book (pages 2-3)

Activity Book (pages 2-3)

National Curriculum Aims
- Understand similarity and difference and use them to draw contrasts.
- Know the history of Britain as a chronological narrative.
- Know and understand significant aspects of the history of the wider world, for example, the expansion of empires.

Introduction

Roman attempts to conquer Britain began in 55 BC with Julius Caesar's unsuccessful invasion. This topic will help pupils to understand the differences between the Romans and the people of Britain at the time of Caesar's invasion. Before pupils read pages 2-3 in the Study Book, it may be helpful to recap what they already know about the Romans and to show them a map of the Roman Empire in the first century BC. Once pupils have read the Study Book pages, discuss the reasons why Caesar's first invasion was unsuccessful. Can pupils think of any ways to overcome the challenges he faced?

Answers to Activity Book Questions

1. Rome: I would be ruled by a dictator.   Britain: I would be ruled by the chief of the tribe.
   Yes — I would pay taxes.   No — I would not pay taxes.
   Yes — there's an army to defend me.   No — there's no army to defend me.

2. E.g. There were lots of grand buildings in Rome — in Britain there weren't any grand buildings. / Rome had a government — in Britain there wasn't a government.

3. Pupils' drawings should show Julius Caesar's ships anchored off shore. Roman soldiers should be jumping off the ships into the sea and wading ashore. More detailed drawings may also show the rough sea and stormy weather.

4. False — True — False — False — True

Extra Activities

- Explain to pupils that many of the buildings in the drawing of Rome on page 2 in the Study Book are still standing. Split the class into groups and ask each group to research a surviving Roman building, e.g. the Colosseum, the Arch of Constantine, the Pantheon. Where is it? When was it built? What was it used for in Roman times? Pupils could produce a tourist pamphlet about their assigned building.

- Explain that some Roman writers claimed Rome conquered countries to bring civilisation to them. Get pupils to compare the pictures of Britain and Rome on page 2 in the Study Book. Why might the Romans have believed that they were more civilised than the Celts?

- Ask pupils the following questions: "Who are we ruled by?" "Do we pay taxes?" "Do we have an army to defend us?" As a class, discuss the similarities and differences between Britain today, and Britain and Rome towards the end of the Iron Age. Is modern Britain more like Rome or Iron Age Britain?

- Ask pupils to write a postcard from Julius Caesar to someone in Rome describing how the invasion of 55 BC went and what Britain was like. Encourage pupils to explore Caesar's feelings about the invasion's outcome.

Discover & Learn British History — Romans in Britain

Trading and Invading

Study Book (pages 4-5)

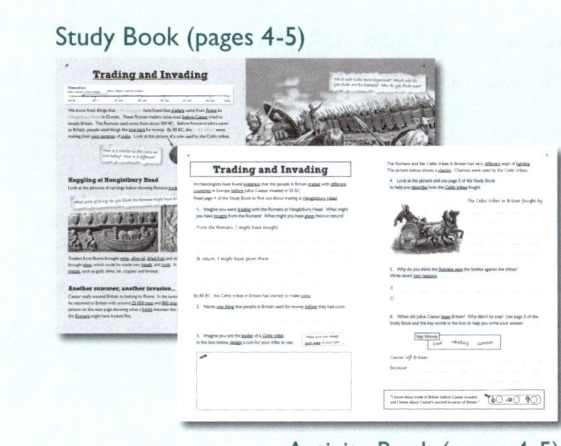

Activity Book (pages 4-5)

National Curriculum Aims

- Know the history of Britain as a chronological narrative.
- Know and understand how Britain has influenced and has been influenced by the wider world.
- Know and understand significant aspects of the history of the wider world, for example, the expansion of empires.

Introduction

Julius Caesar's unsuccessful invasions were one form of contact between late-Iron Age Britain and Rome, but there were also more peaceful contacts in the form of trade. Roman traders brought items to Britain such as wine, olive oil and dried fruit. These military and economic contacts exposed the Celts to Roman culture, and this is reflected in the coins that the Celts produced. Archaeologists have found Celtic coins which are inscribed with Roman-style lettering and use the word 'rex' (meaning 'king' in Latin) to refer to tribal leaders. This indicates that the Romans were already having some influence on Britain even before they successfully invaded.

Answers to Activity Book Questions

1. E.g. *From the Romans, I might have bought* wine / olive oil / glass / luxury foods.
   In return, I might have given them slaves / metals (gold, silver, tin, copper, bronze).
2. iron bars
3. Any appropriate design. If pupils need guidance, encourage them to think about the design of modern coins.
4. E.g. *The Celtic tribes in Britain fought by* swooping in and attacking with their chariots and fast ponies, and then quickly moving away.
5. E.g. The Romans outnumbered the tribes. / The Romans were better equipped than the tribes.
6. *Caesar left Britain* at the end of the summer of 54 BC *because* he had to return to Gaul as the people there were rebelling against him.

Extra Activities

- Ask pupils to write a newspaper report about a battle between the Celtic tribes and the Romans. They could include a picture of the battle, a description of how both sides fought and the outcome of the battle.

- Explain that there have been many other empires throughout history. Split the class into groups and give each group an empire to research, e.g. British, Mongol, Russian. Give each group a world map and ask pupils to colour in the area that their empire ruled over and to find out when their empire began and ended. They should present their map to the class.

- As a class, discuss the items brought to Britain by the Romans that we still use today (e.g. olive oil, wine, glass). Ask pupils to draw pictures to show how we use these things today, e.g. glass is used in windows, olive oil is used in cooking, wine is a popular drink.

Discover & Learn British History — Romans in Britain

Britain Between the Caesars

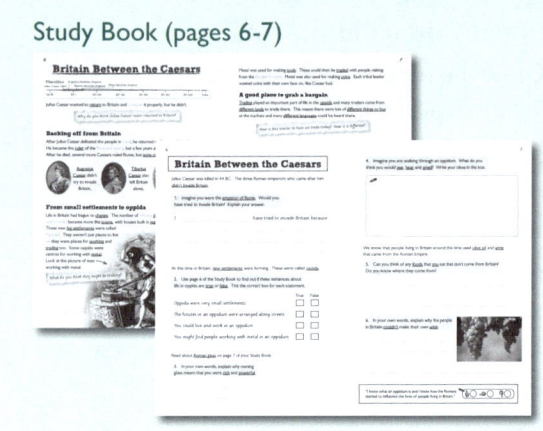

Study Book (pages 6-7)

Activity Book (pages 6-7)

National Curriculum Aims
- Understand change.
- Know and understand how Britain has influenced and has been influenced by the wider world.
- Create structured accounts.

Introduction

Even before much of Britain was successfully conquered by the Romans, there were significant changes in the way the Celts lived. In the late Iron Age, very large, town-like settlements called oppida began to emerge in Britain and mainland Europe. Many archaeologists regard these centres of work, trade and ritual as the earliest examples of urbanism in northern Europe, although this is still debated. What is certain is that oppida represent a major shift in how Iron Age people organised their societies. After reading pages 6-7 in the Study Book, ask pupils whether they think that oppida sound like our towns today. In what ways are they similar or different?

Answers to Activity Book Questions

1. Pupils may answer either way, as long as they give a sensible reason to support their answer.
2. False — True — True — True
3. E.g. Glass was rare and it had to be imported from Rome, so only rich people could afford it.
4. Pupils' answers should show they understand that oppida were places where people lived, worked and traded. Pupils should use information from pages 6-7 in the Study Book, as well as their own imaginations.
5. Any appropriate answer.
6. E.g. Grapes can't grow very well in Britain because it's too cold. Wine is made from grapes, so the people in Britain couldn't make their own wine.

Extra Activities

- Ask pupils to imagine they are going to an oppidum to go shopping. Ask them to write a detailed shopping list describing what they're looking for, why they want these things and who they might buy them from.
- Explain to pupils that the luxury items for sale in oppida could only be bought by the rich and powerful. Ask pupils to think of anything that people buy today to show their status. Why do they think these items are sought after and valued? Do they think it's important to own these items?
- As a class, make a list of fruit and vegetables. Get pupils to research which of these are grown in the UK and which are imported. Encourage pupils to think about the environmental impact of importing food from abroad. Pupils could make a poster persuading people to buy local produce.
- Discuss with pupils how they think the Celts would have responded to the different goods that the Romans brought to Britain such as glass, olive oil and wine. Get pupils to choose one of these goods and make a poster advertising it to the Celts.

Calleva Atrebatum

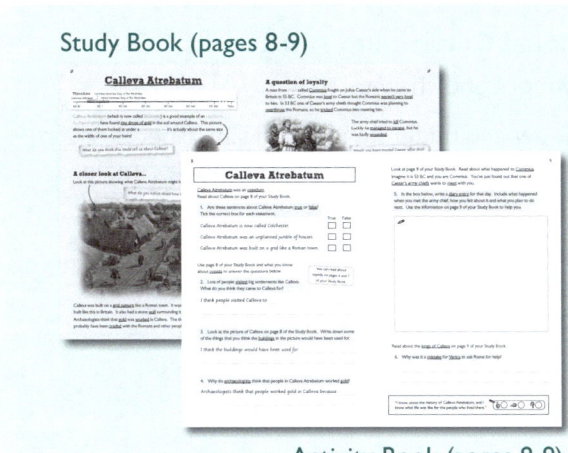

Study Book (pages 8-9)

Activity Book (pages 8-9)

National Curriculum Aims

- Know the history of Britain as a chronological narrative.
- Understand how evidence is used to make historical claims.
- Create structured accounts.
- Understand cause and consequence.

Introduction

In this section, pupils will find out more about what oppida were like by looking at the example of Calleva Atrebatum, the capital of the Atrebates tribe in Britain. The Atrebates share their name with a tribe in Gaul, but the relationship between the two groups is unclear. In the 50s BC, Commius was appointed king of the Gaulish Atrebates by Julius Caesar, following their defeat by the Roman army. However, Commius's relationship with the Romans soon deteriorated. He fought against the Romans in Gaul before eventually fleeing to Britain with a group of loyal followers and becoming ruler of the British Atrebates. Several decades later, one of Commius's successors, Verica, turned back to Rome for military support against the Catuvellauni tribe, giving Emperor Claudius an excuse to invade Britain in AD 43.

Answers to Activity Book Questions

1. False — False — True
2. E.g. *I think people visited Calleva to* buy and sell things.
3. E.g. *I think buildings would have been used for* living in / working with metals in / keeping animals in.
4. *Archaeologists think that people worked gold in Calleva because* they have found tiny drops of gold in the soil.
5. Pupils' answers should show that they understand what happed to Commius when he met with Caesar's army chief, and that Commius might have felt angry and betrayed by Caesar and the Romans. They should also mention Commius' plans to go to Gaul and fight the Romans.
6. E.g. It was a mistake because it gave the Romans an excuse to invade Britain.

Extra Activities

- Split the class into groups and ask them to create a short TV advert which promotes life in Calleva Atrebatum and tries to persuade people to move there. Pupils should research Calleva Atrebatum to help them produce their advert, thinking about the aspects of life there that would most appeal to people.
- Split the class in half and hold a debate about whether the Romans were right to treat Commius in the way that they did. Ask each group to prepare points to back up their argument. After the debate, encourage pupils to think about other ways the army chief could have dealt with the situation in 53 BC.
- Ask pupils to imagine that they are Verica. Get them to write a letter to the Romans asking for help fighting against the Catuvellauni tribe who have just defeated the Atrebates. What could he say to persuade the Romans to come to his aid?

Claudius the Conqueror

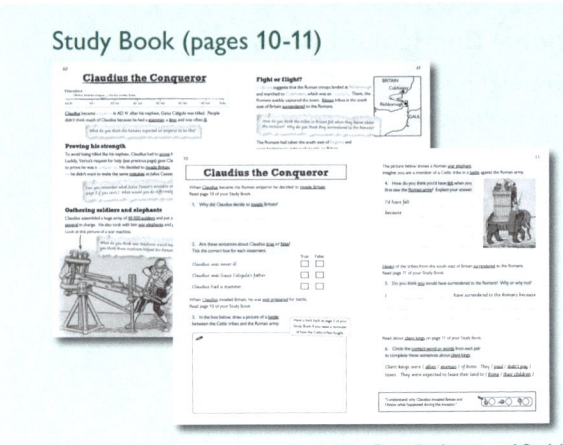

Study Book (pages 10-11)

Activity Book (pages 10-11)

National Curriculum Aims

- Understand change.
- Know and understand significant aspects of the history of the wider world, for example, the expansion of empires.
- Know and use historical terms such as 'client king'.

Introduction

Almost a century after Julius Caesar's failed invasions, the Romans finally gained a foothold in the south-east of Britain thanks to Claudius's campaign, launched in AD 43. Ask pupils to think about what they have learned so far — can they remember what made conquering Britain such an attractive prospect for the Romans? Claudius assembled more soldiers than Caesar used in either of his invasions and took sophisticated war machines and war elephants with him. Get pupils to look at the picture of a war elephant on page 11 in the Activity Book. Do they think the Celts would have seen anything like it before? What sorts of weapons and military equipment might the Celts have had access to. Pupils could look back at the picture on page 5 in the Study Book for ideas. Ask pupils if they're surprised that the Roman invasion was successful. Why or why not?

Answers to Activity Book Questions

1. E.g. He wanted to prove that he was a strong emperor so that he wouldn't be killed.
2. False — False — True
3. Pupils' drawings should show the Romans as a well-organised army with large numbers of men, war machines and war elephants. The tribes should look less organised and they may be using chariots and ponies to attack the Romans. The Romans should look like they are winning.
4. Any appropriate answer and reasoning.
5. Pupils may answer either way, as long as they give a sensible reason to support their answer.
6. *Client kings were* allies *of Rome. They* didn't pay *taxes. They were expected to leave their land to* Rome.

Extra Activities

- There are contrasting accounts of what Claudius was like. Some sources suggest he was ruthless and bloodthirsty, but others say he was too weak to rule. Ask pupils to discuss how both these sides of him come through in the story of his conquest of Britain. Get pupils to find out more about Claudius's career and produce a character profile describing the two sides to his personality. Pupils should back up each trait with examples.

- Get pupils to research Roman war machines. What materials were used to make them? How did they work? They should draw a diagram of a war machine and label it with the information they have found.

- Ask pupils to think about the relationship between client kings and the Romans. They could produce a table listing the advantages and disadvantages of client kingship for both the Romans and the client kings.

Discover & Learn British History — Romans in Britain

The Roman Army

Study Book (pages 12-13)

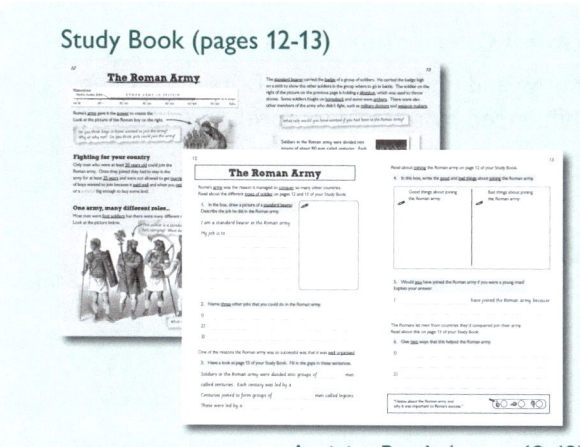

Activity Book (pages 12-13)

National Curriculum Aims

- Know and understand significant aspects of the history of the wider world, for example, the expansion of empires.

- Understand the connection between military and cultural history.

Introduction

At its height, the Roman army may have had around half a million members. This massive, versatile and hugely powerful force was a major factor underpinning the might of the Roman Empire. Roman soldiers were very well trained and highly disciplined. Soldiers who refused to follow orders were subjected to harsh punishments and could even be sentenced to death. When soldiers weren't training or fighting, they also built forts and roads, and policed the lands they had conquered. Once pupils have read pages 12-13 in the Study Book, discuss the roles played by Roman soldiers. Are there any similarities with the work of modern armies? What are the differences?

Answers to Activity Book Questions

1. Any appropriate drawing. E.g. *My job is to* carry the badge for my group of soldiers. The badge is on a stick and I carry it high in the air to show the soldiers where to go in battle.

2. E.g. foot soldier / archer / doctor / weapon maker / centurion / legate

3. *Soldiers in the Roman army were divided into groups of* about 80 *men called centuries. Each century was led by a* centurion. *Centuries joined to form groups of* about 5000 *men called legions. These were led by a* legate.

4. E.g. Good things about joining the Roman army: paid well / given land on retirement / given a pension
   Bad things about joining the Roman army: had to stay in the army for 25 years / couldn't get married / might die in battle

5. Pupils may answer either way, as long as they give a sensible reason to support their answer.

6. E.g. It gave the army new troops for the battlefield. / It kept the young men busy so they didn't try to rebel.

Extra Activities

- Assign each pupil a piece of equipment that a Roman soldier would have used (e.g. sword, javelin, armour, helmet). Ask pupils to find out what their piece of equipment was made from and what it was used for. Pupils should then make a replica of their equipment out of cardboard and write the information they have found out about it on a piece of paper. The replicas and information can then be made into a class display.

- Show pupils examples of the badges used to represent different legions in the Roman army. Pupils could then design a badge to represent their class, school or family.

- Remind pupils that auxiliary troops in the Roman army gained the right to become Roman citizens at the end of their service. Discuss with pupils what it means to be a citizen today. How do people become citizens of Britain? What rights and responsibilities do British citizens have?

Building Roads to Conquer

Study Book (pages 14-15)

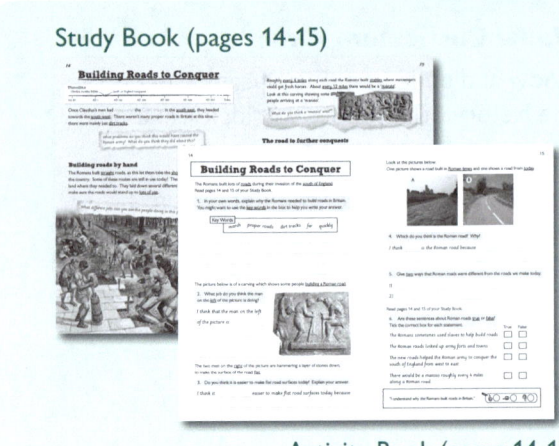

Activity Book (pages 14-15)

National Curriculum Aims
- Know and understand how Britain has been influenced by the wider world.
- Understand similarity and difference and use them to draw contrasts.
- Understand change.

Introduction

As well as being world leaders in military strength, the Romans also made important advances in technology and engineering. By the end of the first century, they had built over 8000 miles of road in Britain — enough to stretch from Land's End to John O'Groats more than nine times. Wherever possible, these Roman roads were remarkably straight, although they did zigzag up hills to make climbing them easier. These roads were a key factor in the Romans' military success — by enabling their troops to move quickly and extensively, roads helped the Romans to conquer and control their vast empire. Roads also had an important economic role, facilitating the movement and trade of goods throughout the empire.

Answers to Activity Book Questions

1. E.g. Before the Romans came to Britain the roads were mostly dirt tracks. The Romans couldn't march very far or very quickly on these tracks, so they needed to build proper roads.
2. E.g. *I think that the man on the left of the picture is* carrying a bucket of stones that will be used to build the road.
3. E.g *I think it is easier to make flat road surfaces today because* we have machinery that we can use to help us.
4. E.g. *I think* A *is the Roman road because* it's straight and it's made of stone slabs.
5. E.g. They were straight. / They were made by hand. / They were made of stone slabs.
6. True — True — False —False

Extra Activities

- Split the class into pairs. Ask one pupil in each pair to take on the role of a television news reporter and the other pupil to take on the role of a Roman soldier building a Roman road. Each pair should act out an interview. Why is the road being built? What will the benefits of the road be? How is the soldier building it? Is it hard work? Would the soldier rather be working on the road or fighting battles?
- With the whole class, discuss why pupils think roads aren't always built in a straight line, e.g. to go up hills, to avoid barriers like mountain ranges and lakes. Then discuss why pupils think it was more important for the Romans to have straight roads than it is for us today.
- Explain to pupils that some of our modern roads follow old Roman roads, such as Ermine Street, Watling Street and Fosse Way. Ask pupils to research these roads and produce a map showing them. They could also include any place names with Roman origins along the roads.

The Invasion Continues...

Study Book (pages 16-17)

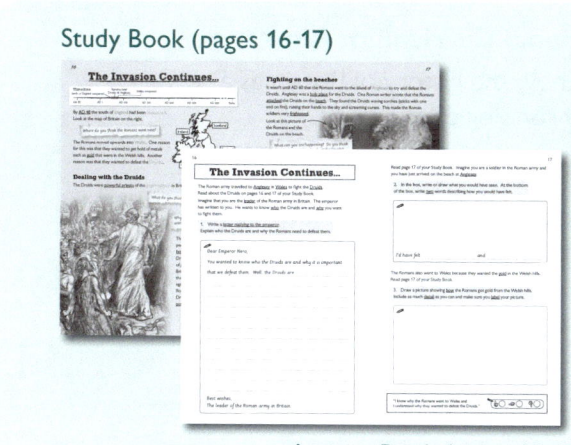

Activity Book (pages 16-17)

National Curriculum Aims

- Know the history of Britain as a chronological narrative.
- Know and understand how Britain has been influenced by the wider world.
- Know and understand the connection between military and religious history.

Introduction

This topic will show pupils how the Romans continued to increase their power in Britain by defeating the Druids in Wales. As spiritual leaders, the Druids were powerful and commanded a great deal of respect. However, their religious beliefs were rejected by the Romans, who believed that they performed evil magic and human sacrifice. The Romans were also aware that Anglesey, where the Druids were based, offered refuge to people who were fleeing Roman rule. Defeat of the Druids would, therefore, prevent them becoming the focus of anti-Roman resistance. It would also enable the Romans to exploit the gold resources in Wales. While the Romans were successful in suppressing Druidism, the religion was revived in Britain in the 18th century and there are still people who practise it today. After pupils have read pages 16-17 in the Study Book, ask them if they can remember what the Romans used gold for. Why might they have wanted access to more gold?

Answers to Activity Book Questions

1. Pupils' letters should be written in the first person and draw on information from the Study Book to explain who the Druids were and why the Romans needed to defeat them.

2. Answers should include Druids on a beach carrying flaming torches and raising their arms in the air. They may also include the Druids' sacred trees. Pupils should have written two words to describe how they would have felt.

3. Pupils' drawings should show an aqueduct carrying water to the top of a hill to fill up large water tanks. They should also show waves of water pouring down the hill from the tanks and soil being washed away to reveal the gold. Each part of the drawing should be labelled.

Extra Activities

- Get pupils to research the Druids and find one fact about them, e.g. they weren't just priests, they also acted as judges and teachers. Bring the class back together to discuss the pupils' findings. You could write all the facts down on the whiteboard or on a large piece of paper.

- As a class, discuss why pupils think the Druids had so much influence over the people of Britain. They should then write a short paragraph explaining why the Romans wouldn't have liked this.

- Get pupils to research Roman aqueducts. What were they for? How were they constructed? How did they work? Pupils should draw an aqueduct and label it with the information they have found.

- Ask pupils to write a short diary entry, imagining that they are a Roman mining for gold in Wales. Encourage them to write about the processes involved in mining the gold. They should also think about whether it was hard work and how they might have felt when they saw the gold.

Discover & Learn British History — Romans in Britain

Turning Britain into Rome

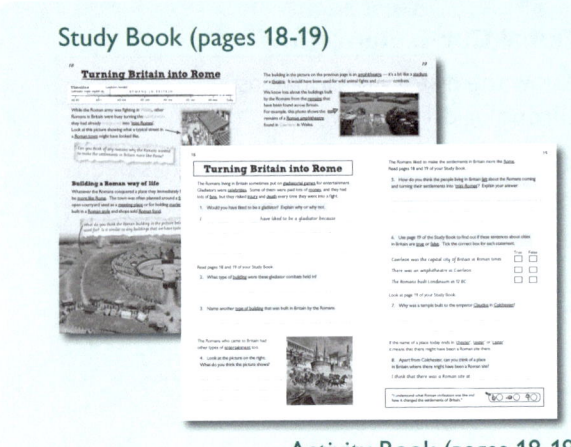

Study Book (pages 18-19)

Activity Book (pages 18-19)

National Curriculum Aims

- Know the history of Britain as a chronological narrative.
- Understand change.
- Know and understand how Britain has been influenced by the wider world.

Introduction

The Romans built the first proper towns in Britain and linked them with their impressive roads. They based these towns on Rome itself, and each town had a similar layout, with streets and buildings organised in a grid-like pattern. The Romans also brought their own forms of entertainment with them to Britain, such as gladiatorial games. All of this was a way of establishing Roman power — by creating 'mini Romes' in Britain, the Romans strengthened their dominance over British society and culture. After pupils have read pages 18-19 in the Study Book, ask them to look back to the drawing of Rome on page 2. How does the picture of a Roman settlement on page 18 compare to it? Can they see any similarities?

Answers to Activity Book Questions

1. Pupils may answer either way, as long as they give a sensible reason to support their answer.
2. amphitheatres
3. E.g. temples / shops / villas / public baths / forts
4. E.g. It shows people racing in chariots that are being pulled by horses.
5. Any appropriate answer. Pupils should give a sensible reason to support their answer.
6. False — True — False
7. E.g. Claudius successfully conquered Colchester and when he died the Romans worshipped him as a god.
8. E.g. Manchester / Leicester / Lancaster / Chester / Worcester

Extra Activities

- Split the class into groups and ask them to use the internet to find out more about gladiators. How did people become gladiators? What exactly did they do? Were they important people? Each group could produce a short presentation to share their findings with the rest of the class.

- Show pupils pictures of Roman amphitheatres and modern stadiums. Ask them to identify similarities and differences between them. Then get them to imagine attending an event in an amphitheatre and ask them to produce a piece of descriptive writing about how it would feel. What would the atmosphere be like? Would they be excited? What would they be able to see and hear?

- Ask pupils to name features of their nearest town, e.g. churches, shops, markets, sports venues, swimming pools, theatres. Ask pupils if they think there would have been anything equivalent to these in Roman settlements. Do they think they would have liked to live in a Roman settlement?

Discover & Learn British History — Romans in Britain

Boudica Bites Back

Study Book (pages 20-21)

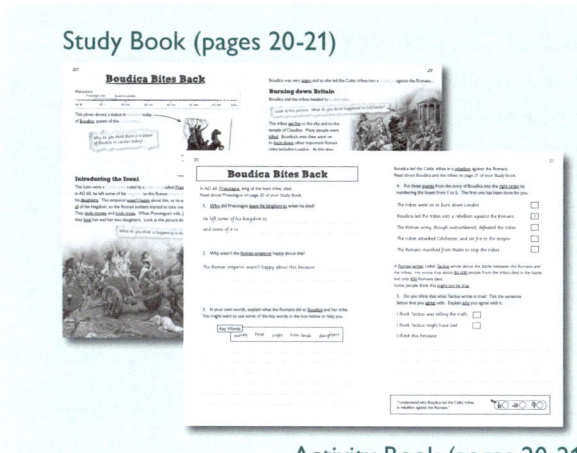

Activity Book (pages 20-21)

National Curriculum Aims

- Know the history of Britain as a chronological narrative.
- Create structured accounts.
- Understand why there are different interpretations of the past.
- Know how people's lives have shaped Britain.

Introduction

Boudica is one of the most famous women in British history. She rebelled against the Romans, successfully leading several Celtic tribes in attacks on the major Roman cities of Colchester, London and St Albans. Boudica's revolt took the Romans by surprise and was brutal in its nature — towns were completely destroyed and the inhabitants killed. The main reason for Boudica's initial success, however, was that most of the Roman army was still in Wales fighting the Druids. When Roman reinforcements arrived, the Celts were defeated. Although Boudica's revolt ultimately failed, she still has a reputation as a fierce warrior. Her actions show that women could be leaders in Iron Age Britain, in contrast to the women of Rome who were largely confined to the home. Before pupils read pages 20-21 in the Study Book, show them some paintings or drawings of Boudica. What impression do they get of her from these images?

Answers to Activity Book Questions

1. *He left some of his kingdom to* the Roman emperor *and some of it to* his daughters.

2. E.g. *The Roman emperor wasn't happy about this because* he was expecting to inherit all of the kingdom and not just part of it.

3. Pupils' answers should use information from the Study Book to explain what the Roman soldiers took from the Iceni tribe and what they did to Boudica and her daughters.

4. 3 — 1 — 5 — 2 — 4

5. Pupils may choose either sentence, as long as they give a sensible reason to support their choice.

Extra Activities

- Ask pupils to write a newspaper article reporting on Boudica's rebellion against the Romans. They should describe where the rebels went and what they did there. They could also include made-up quotes from Boudica about her reasons for leading the rebellion and what she hoped to achieve.

- Ask pupils to share their answers to question 5 in the Activity Book and discuss why it is important to think about the reliability of evidence. Introduce the idea of bias. Do pupils think Tacitus was biased? Suggest some theoretical sources relating to Boudica, e.g. an eyewitness account of Boudica's attack on Colchester, Boudica's diary, a photograph of Colchester after the attack. How reliable would such sources be? Might they be biased towards one side or the other?

- Get pupils to produce a storyboard about Boudica's rebellion. Tell them to split the storyboard into seven sections, starting with the death of Prasutagus and ending with Boudica's defeat.

Discover & Learn British History — Romans in Britain

Towards Scotland

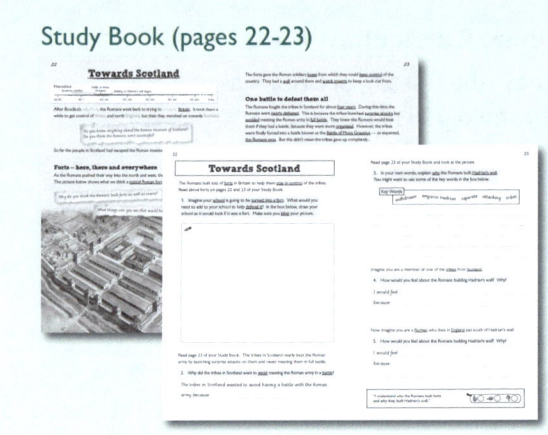

Study Book (pages 22-23)

Activity Book (pages 22-23)

National Curriculum Aims

- Know the history of Britain as a chronological narrative.
- Understand cause and consequence.
- Create structured accounts.

Introduction

Scotland (or Caledonia as it was called by the Romans) provided another opportunity for Roman expansion. The Romans eventually managed to defeat the Scottish tribes at the Battle of Mons Graupius, but despite this victory they were still unable to take complete control of Scotland. Some Scottish tribes continued to attack the Romans and, ultimately, their guerrilla tactics proved too difficult to deal with. As the empire became involved in more important military campaigns elsewhere, it was no longer worth the Romans' while to try and subdue the tribes. As a result, Scotland never became part of Roman Britain, and the Romans didn't build towns and roads there in the same way that they did in England and Wales. Instead, the Romans built Hadrian's wall to protect Roman Britain and keep the Scottish tribes out.

Answers to Activity Book Questions

1. Pupils' drawings should show a high wall surrounding the school with watch towers for keeping a lookout. The drawings should be labelled.

2. E.g. *The tribes in Scotland wanted to avoid having a battle with the Roman army because* they knew they would be beaten as the Roman army was more organised.

3. E.g. The tribes of Scotland kept attacking the Romans even after they had been beaten. The Roman army was gradually withdrawn from Scotland and Emperor Hadrian decided it was best to build a wall across the top of the Roman land to separate it from Scotland.

4. Any appropriate answer. Pupils must give a sensible reason to support their answer.

5. Any appropriate answer. Pupils must give a sensible reason to support their answer.

Extra Activities

- The remains of Roman forts can be found across Britain. Ask pupils to identify the fort nearest to where they live and then make a poster about it. They could draw a picture of the fort in the middle of the page and label it with information, e.g. buildings that would have made up the fort such as barracks and hospitals, its defensive features such as ditches and ramparts, the sort of building materials that were used.

- Ask pupils to imagine they are a general in the Roman army. Ask them to write a diary entry describing how they feel about the Scottish tribes. How did they feel when they defeated the tribes at the Battle of Mons Graupius? Were they frustrated that the tribes carried on attacking them after the battle?

- Hold a class debate about whether the Romans were right to retreat from Scotland. What would pupils have done if they were in charge of the Roman army?

Building Hadrian's Wall

Study Book (pages 24-25)

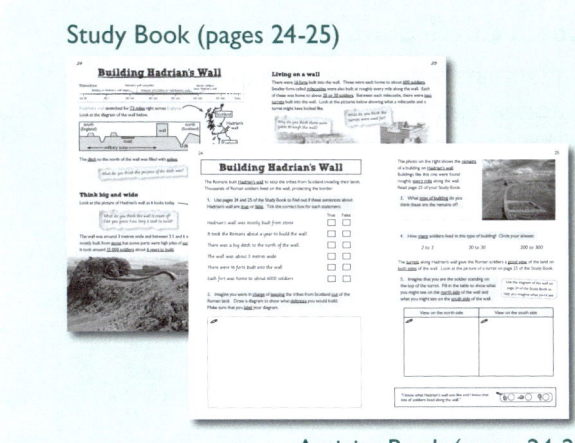

Activity Book (pages 24-25)

National Curriculum Aims

- Know the history of Britain as a chronological narrative.

- Know and understand how Britain has been influenced by the wider world.

- Know and understand significant aspects of the history of the wider world, for example, the expansion of empires.

Introduction

Work on Hadrian's wall started on the orders of Emperor Hadrian in AD 122. As well as providing military defence, the wall enabled the Romans to police and protect Roman Britain by allowing them to monitor who came into the empire from Scotland and who left. It also gave them the opportunity to collect taxes from those who wanted to cross the border. Today, there are several well-preserved sites along the wall. Wallsend features a reconstruction of part of the wall and Housesteads is one of the best-preserved forts, with the foundations of a hospital and barracks still visible. After pupils have read pages 24-25 in the Study Book, show them some pictures of Wallsend and Housesteads so they have an idea what the forts and the wall would have looked like. Then ask pupils to look back at the diagram of the wall on page 24. Why do they think the wall was effective?

Answers to Activity Book Questions

1. True — False — True — True — True — False

2. Pupils' diagrams should be labelled and show defences that would be strong enough to keep out the attacking tribes. They may be historically accurate or more inventive.

3. a milecastle

4. Pupils should have circled: 20 to 30.

5. E.g. *View on the north side*: I'd see a big ditch with spikes and then a mound.
   View on the south side: I'd see a road running along the wall, then two mounds with a small ditch between them.

Extra Activities

- Assign each pupil the role of either a Roman leader, a Roman soldier, a person living near Hadrian's wall or a trader. Ask pupils to write down what their character might have thought of the wall. Do they think it is a good idea? How is it impacting on their lives? As a class, discuss what pupils have written.

- Split pupils into groups and assign each group another famous wall from history, e.g. the Great Wall of China, the Berlin Wall. Ask them to find similarities and differences between their wall and Hadrian's wall, e.g. when and where they were built, why they were built, what they were built from.

- Divide pupils into groups to make a model of the wall. Pupils could make models of forts, milecastles, turrets and the wall itself. They could then combine their models, with the milecastles evenly spaced along the wall and two turrets placed between each milecastle. The forts could be placed anywhere along the wall.

Discover & Learn British History — Romans in Britain

Life at the Edge of the Empire

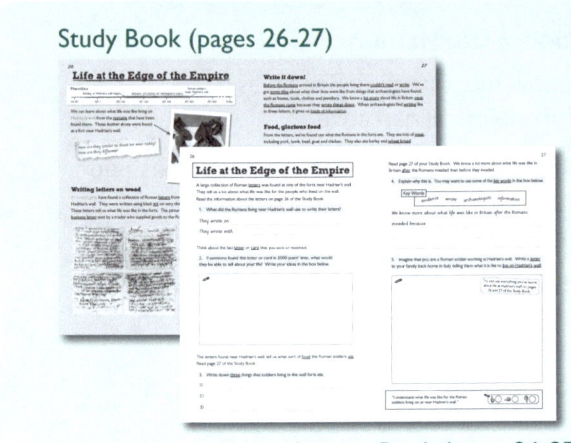

Study Book (pages 26-27)

Activity Book (pages 26-27)

National Curriculum Aims
- Understand how evidence is used to make historical claims.
- Create structured accounts.
- Understand the connection between military and social history.

Introduction

A huge variety of artefacts, from combs and hairpins to swords and lances, have been found along Hadrian's wall, giving us valuable insights into Roman life in Britain. The wall was clearly very important to the Romans. It was actively used for 300 years and soldiers from across the empire were stationed there. Forts were built along the length of the wall and each one was home to an auxiliary unit. A unit could contain up to 1000 soldiers — so Hadrian's wall was home to a lot of people. Cold winters and the constant threat of attack might not have been too enjoyable, but the Romans soon built settlements just outside of their forts. These settlements featured public baths, shops, temples, workshops and taverns where the soldiers could enjoy good food and have fun. Before pupils read pages 26-27 in the Study Book, ask them what they think life as a soldier on Hadrian's wall would have been like. What might they have done every day?

Answers to Activity Book Questions

1. *They wrote on* thin pieces of wood.
   They wrote with black ink.
2. Any appropriate answer.
3. E.g. meat / pork / lamb / beef / goat / chicken / barley / wheat bread
4. E.g. *We know more about what life was like after the Romans invaded because* the Romans wrote things down. When archaeologists find this evidence, they can get lots of information.
5. Pupils' letters should be written in the first person. Pupils should use as much information from pages 26-27 in the Study Book as possible, as well as their own imaginations.

Extra Activities

- Split pupils into small groups and ask them to act out things a Roman soldier on Hadrian's wall may have done, e.g. keeping watch from the turrets, visiting a shop, having a bath, going to a tavern. The groups could take it in turns to act out an activity while the rest of the class tries to guess what it is.

- Using information from page 27 in the Study Book, ask pupils to write a menu for a Roman soldier for a day, and then write a menu for themselves. As a class, discuss the similarities and differences between what we eat today and what Roman soldiers ate.

- Get pupils to write out their letters from page 27 in the Activity Book so that they look like those found near Hadrian's wall. If thin pieces of wood are not available, they could use a wet tea bag to stain some paper to create an aged effect. Once the paper is dry, they can use black ink to write on it.

Discover & Learn British History — Romans in Britain

The Roman North

Study Book (pages 28-29)

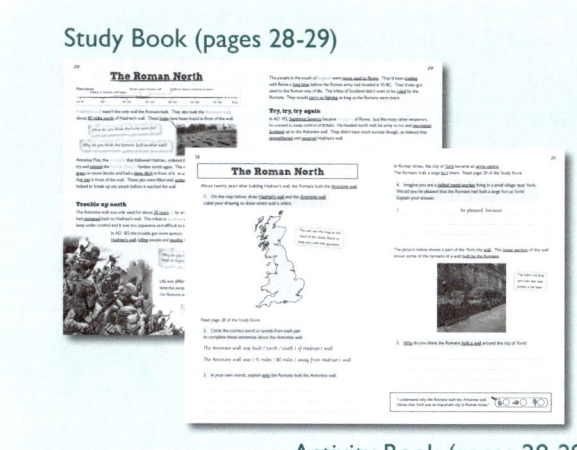

Activity Book (pages 28-29)

National Curriculum Aims

- Know the history of Britain as a chronological narrative.
- Know and understand significant aspects of the history of the wider world, for example, the expansion of empires.
- Know and understand how Britain has been influenced by the wider world.

Introduction

Under Hadrian's successor, Antoninus Pius, the Romans tried once again to extend their border northwards into Scotland. Pius's forces successfully invaded the Scottish Lowlands, and in AD 142 they began work on the Antonine wall, 80 miles north of Hadrian's wall. This campaign achieved a modest territorial expansion, but some historians suggest its primary purpose may have been to shore up Pius's position in Rome by providing him with a notable military achievement that would demonstrate his strength. While the wall may have achieved this short-term goal, it didn't succeed in quelling the tribes and asserting Roman control over Scotland — it was abandoned after about 20 years due to continued attacks. After pupils have read pages 28-29 in the Study Book, ask them why they think the tribes of Scotland didn't want to be ruled by the Romans.

Answers to Activity Book Questions

1. Pupils should have drawn the Antonine wall running roughly from Old Kilpatrick near Glasgow to Bo'ness near Edinburgh. They should have drawn Hadrian's wall running roughly from Bowness-on-Solway to Wallsend near Newcastle.

2. *The Antonine wall was built* north *of Hadrian's wall. The Antonine wall was* 80 miles *away from Hadrian's wall.*

3. E.g. The Romans built the Antonine wall to try and extend the empire further north again. They wanted to claim more of Scotland.

4. Pupils may answer either way, as long as they give a sensible reason to support their answer.

5. Pupils should use the information on pages 28-29 in the Study Book to explain why a wall might have been built.

Extra Activities

- Ask pupils to research the Antonine wall. They should find out about how the wall was constructed, what life was like on the wall and what remains for people to see today. They could use their research to produce a tourist leaflet that will encourage people to visit the Antonine wall.

- Ask pupils to imagine being the chief of a Scottish tribe. They should write a speech to give to their tribe just before they launch an attack on the Romans. Pupils should think about how the tribes felt towards the Romans and how they could prepare their tribesmen for the battle.

- Discuss with pupils how they think Roman leaders might have felt about their repeated failures to conquer Scotland. What might it suggest about Roman power? Might these failures have affected how confident Roman leaders would have felt about trying to conquer other places?

Discover & Learn British History — Romans in Britain

Living Like a Roman

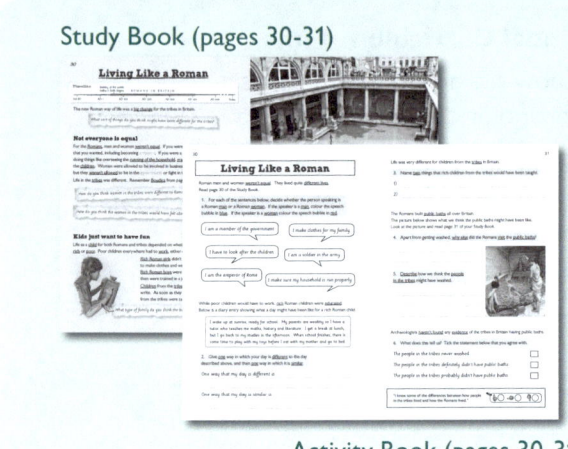

Study Book (pages 30-31)

Activity Book (pages 30-31)

National Curriculum Aims

- Know and understand how Britain has been influenced by the wider world.
- Understand similarity and difference and use them to draw contrasts.
- Understand how evidence is used to make historical claims.

Introduction

This topic gives pupils the opportunity to explore aspects of everyday life for Romans in Britain, and to draw comparisons between the lifestyles of the Romans and the tribes. After pupils have read pages 30-31 in the Study Book, ask them to think about how the tribes would have reacted to the social and cultural changes introduced by the Romans. As a class, discuss which changes might have been the most significant. Do pupils think the tribes might have embraced any of the changes? Do they think some people would have been more receptive to Roman influence than others? Why?

Answers to Activity Book Questions

1. Pupils should have coloured the following sentences blue:
   I am a member of the government.
   I am a soldier in the army.
   I am the emperor of Rome.
   The other sentences should be coloured red.

2. Pupils should compare their own day with the day described in the diary entry.

3. E.g. They would have been taught how to fight. / They would have been taught how to hunt.

4. E.g. To meet with friends. / To catch up on the latest news. / To socialise.

5. E.g. We think that the people in the tribes used soap to wash themselves in rivers or streams.

6. Pupils should have ticked: The people in the tribes probably didn't have public baths.

Extra Activities

- As a class, discuss whether pupils are surprised by the things Roman women were not allowed to do. Would they rather be a woman living in Roman society or in a tribe? Discuss how the lives of Roman women were different from the lives of women in Britain today.

- Split the class into three groups. The first group should pretend to be rich Roman girls, the second rich Roman boys and the third children from a tribe. Ask each group to act out a scene as their characters. As a class, discuss the lives of all three characters. Which one would pupils prefer to be and why?

- Ask pupils to imagine that they are a Roman who has just opened some public baths in Britain. Get them to design a poster to advertise their baths. They could include pictures of their baths, describe their features and explain why people might want to visit them. Pupils could research the meaning of the following words and use them in their posters: 'palaestra' (exercise area), 'apodyterium' (changing room), 'frigidarium' (cold bath), 'tepidarium' (warm room), 'caldarium' (hot room), 'strigil' (a curved tool used to clean the skin).

Living in Luxury Villas

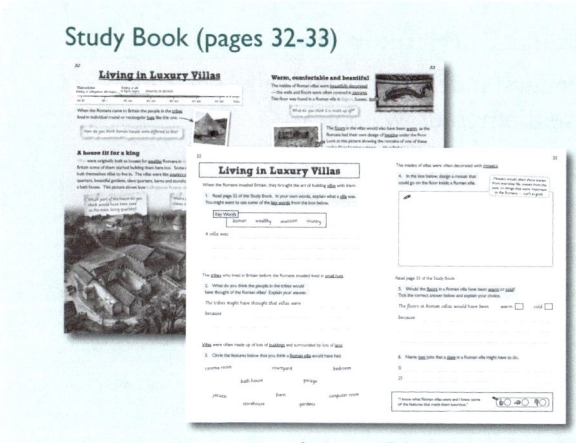

Study Book (pages 32-33)

Activity Book (pages 32-33)

National Curriculum Aims

- Understand how evidence is used to make historical claims.
- Know and understand how Britain has been influenced by the wider world.
- Know and use historical terms such as 'hypocaust'.

Introduction

As well as bringing their towns and forms of entertainment to Britain, the Romans also brought their houses. The villas that wealthy Romans built in Britain were grand, sophisticated buildings made from stone. They had underfloor heating and were decorated with marble and mosaics. These Roman villas were very different from the simple houses built by members of the British tribes. Often referred to as roundhouses, these one-room huts were made of wattle and daub — wood, clay and straw. After pupils have read pages 32-33 in the Study Book, make sure they understand that it was only the very wealthy who lived in villas — poorer Romans would have had much simpler homes. As a class, discuss the features of Roman villas. Are pupils surprised that people living 2000 years ago had underfloor heating? What other features did Roman villas have that our houses still have today? Would pupils be comfortable living in a Roman villa? What features of their own homes would they miss?

Answers to Activity Book Questions

1. E.g. *A villa was* a large house built for a wealthy Roman. Villas are a bit like the country mansions that we have today.
2. Any appropriate answer. Pupils should give a sensible reason to support their answer.
3. Pupils should have circled: bath house / courtyard / bedroom / barn / storehouse / gardens.
4. Any appropriate design.
5. Warm. E.g. The villas often had an underfloor heating system called a hypocaust.
6. E.g. cook meals / collect wood to put in the furnace

Extra Activities

- Ask pupils to imagine they are an estate agent trying to sell a Roman villa. They should create an advert that will persuade people to buy the villa. Their advert should include pictures of the villa and a description of its rooms, decoration and other features.

- Get pupils to make the mosaic that they designed for question 4 in the Activity Book (more complicated designs may need to be simplified). Pupils will need to draw out a plan of their mosaic onto a base of thick card. They can then use glue to stick ready-prepared coloured squares of paper or card onto the base.

- Ask pupils to imagine they are a slave working in a Roman villa. They should research the different tasks slaves were given, then write a diary entry describing the things they would have to do throughout the day. They could also include how they felt about each task.

Discover & Learn British History — Romans in Britain

Religion in Roman Britain

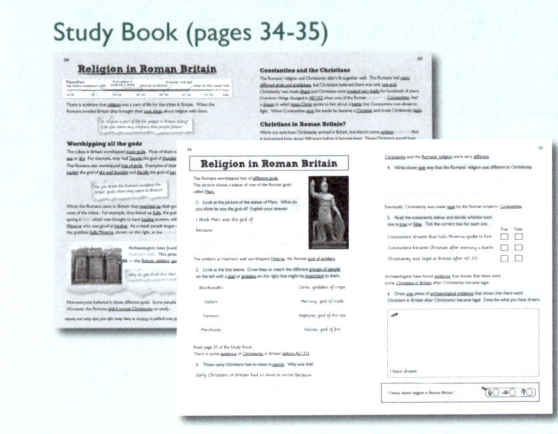

Study Book (pages 34-35)

Activity Book (pages 34-35)

National Curriculum Aims
- Understand similarity and difference and use them to draw contrasts.
- Understand how evidence is used to make historical claims.
- Understand the connection between religious and cultural history.
- Know and understand how Britain has been influenced by the wider world.

Introduction

Religion was an important part of Roman society. In addition to their 12 main gods and goddesses, the Romans worshipped many more who were linked to everything from forests to keys. As the empire expanded, the Romans adopted gods from places they conquered. This was especially the case if they had been impressed with how the conquered people had fought — they thought a powerful god must have been helping them. However, Christianity was one religion the Romans didn't embrace so readily. They didn't like the fact that Christians refused to worship Roman gods and the Roman emperor, so they banned Christianity and persecuted its followers. In spite of this, Christianity continued to grow and it eventually achieved acceptance when Emperor Constantine made it legal in AD 313. Christianity became the official religion of the Roman Empire in AD 380, but paganism remained popular in many places, including in Britain.

Answers to Activity Book Questions

1. E.g. *I think Mars was the god of* war *because* he is dressed in armour and is holding a shield.
2. Blacksmiths — Vulcan, god of fire Farmers — Ceres, goddess of crops
   Sailors — Neptune, god of the sea Merchants — Mercury, god of trade
3. E.g. *Early Christians in Britain had to meet in secret because* otherwise they might have been punished for their beliefs. / Christianity was illegal until AD 313.
4. E.g. The Romans' religion had several gods and goddesses, but the Christians believed in just one god.
5. False — True — False
6. Pupils should have drawn either the mosaic of Jesus Christ from Hinton St Mary, or the lead tank with some of the letters of the word 'Christ', from Icklingham. They should have described what they have drawn.

Extra Activities

- Split the class into small groups and assign each group a Roman god or goddess to research, e.g. Mercury, Saturn, Venus, Minerva. Pupils should produce a fact file on their god which could cover their role, their powers, their relationship to other gods, etc. The fact files could be collected and made into a class book.
- Ask pupils to pick a group of people (e.g. teachers, footballers, astronauts) and design a Roman god or goddess for them to worship. Pupils should draw and label their deity and give them a name.
- Discuss with the class aspects of Christianity, e.g. everyone being equal before God, salvation and life after death. Ask pupils why they think this might have made Christianity attractive to people in the Roman Empire.

Trouble in the Empire

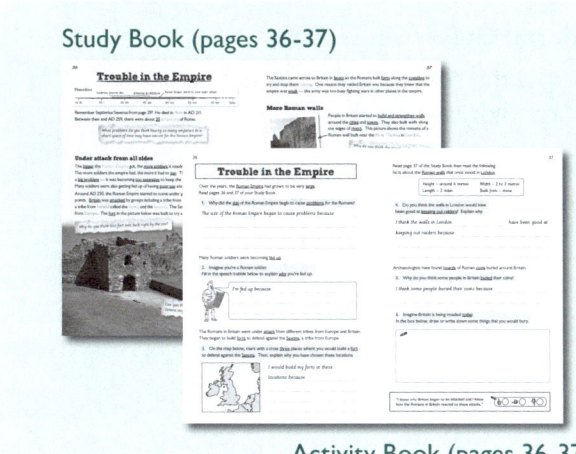

Study Book (pages 36-37)

Activity Book (pages 36-37)

National Curriculum Aims

- Know the history of Britain as a chronological narrative.
- Know and understand significant aspects of the history of the wider world, for example, the dissolution of empires.
- Understand cause and consequence.

Introduction

From the third century AD, weaknesses were emerging throughout the Roman Empire — and Roman Britain was no different. Centuries of successful expansion became part of the empire's undoing as its vast territory became increasingly difficult to govern and hugely expensive to maintain. These problems were exacerbated by unstable leadership as emperors came and went in quick succession, partly as a result of frequent assassinations. Increasing external attacks on the empire only made matters worse. After pupils have read pages 36-37 in the Study Book, ask them how they think the Romans might have felt about facing war on three different fronts in Britain — from the Picts, the Scots and the Saxons. Then discuss how trouble in the empire would have affected daily life for people in Britain.

Answers to Activity Book Questions

1. E.g. *The size of the Roman Empire began to cause problems because* it had grown so big that it needed more soldiers, but it couldn't afford to pay all the soldiers it needed to defend it.

2. E.g. *I'm fed up because* I'm fighting to protect the empire, but I'm not getting paid enough money or being given enough food.

3. Pupils should have drawn 3 crosses on the coastline of Britain.
   E.g. *I would build my forts in these locations because* the Saxons travelled from Europe to Britain by boat, so my forts would help stop them coming ashore.

4. Pupils may answer either way, as long as they give a sensible reason to support their answer.

5. E.g. *I think some people buried their coins because* they were feeling scared and wanted to protect their money.

6. Pupils should have drawn or written some things that are important to them, and that are suitable to be buried.

Extra Activities

- Ask pupils to write a story about a person in fourth century Britain who has to bury their coins. Why are they burying their coins? Where are they going to bury them? Do they expect to retrieve them one day?

- Split the class into three groups and ask each group to research either the Picts, the Scots or the Saxons. They should think about where they came from, their way of life, where and when they attacked Britain, etc. Each group should put together a short presentation on their topic, then share it with the rest of the class.

- In pairs, get pupils to write a conversation between two Roman generals about the problems they were facing in Britain. How were they feeling? Were they starting to panic? Were their defences working? What did they think they should do next?

Discover & Learn British History — Romans in Britain

The Romans Retreat

Study Book (pages 38-39)

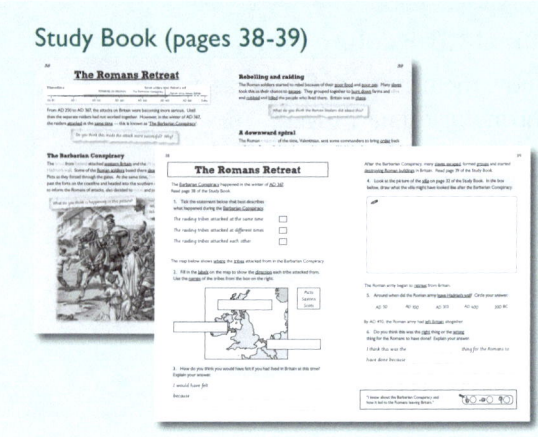

Activity Book (pages 38-39)

National Curriculum Aims

- Know the history of Britain as a chronological narrative.
- Know and understand significant aspects of the history of the wider world, for example, the dissolution of empires.
- Understand cause and consequence.

Introduction

In this topic, pupils will learn how and why Roman rule in Britain came to an end. From around AD 367, the situation in Britain deteriorated as the Picts, the Scots and the Saxons began to mount more coordinated raids. At the same time, other parts of the Roman Empire, including Italy, were also suffering serious attacks, and at the start of the fifth century AD, soldiers were withdrawn from Britain to fight in mainland Europe. In AD 410, Rome was sacked — this was the first time in 800 years that the city had been invaded by a foreign force. As a result, when Britain called on Rome for military support, Emperor Honorius had nothing to offer. He told the British people they would have to defend themselves, and this marked the end of Britain's relationship with Rome.

Answers to Activity Book Questions

1. Pupils should have ticked: The raiding tribes attacked at the same time.
2. From north to south, students should have labelled: Picts — Scots — Saxons.
3. Any appropriate answer. Pupils should give a sensible reason to support their answer.
4. Pupils' drawings should show the villa on page 32 in the Study Book either on fire or burnt down. They might also have included groups of slaves robbing the villa and attacking people.
5. Pupils should have circled: AD 400.
6. Pupils may answer either way, as long as they give a sensible reason to support their answer.

Extra Activities

- As a class, make a list of reasons why the Roman Empire was falling apart. Ask pupils to imagine that they are Emperor Honorius. Challenge them to come up with three things they would have done to resolve the empire's problems and prevent its collapse.
- Ask for volunteers to take on the characters of people in Britain in the early fifth century AD, such as a Roman soldier, a slave, a spy and an invader. Get the rest of the class to ask them questions about the situation in Britain. Why did they act in the way they did? What are they unhappy about? Are they worried about the future? What are they planning to do next?
- Ask pupils to produce a timeline to consolidate their knowledge about the Romans in Britain. They should use the information and timelines throughout the Study Book to pick out the most important events during the Roman occupation.
- Hold a class debate about the impact the Romans had on Britain. Half the class should argue that the Romans had a positive impact on Britain and the other half should argue that they had a negative impact.

Discover & Learn British History — Romans in Britain

The Fall of the Roman Empire

Study Book (pages 2-3)

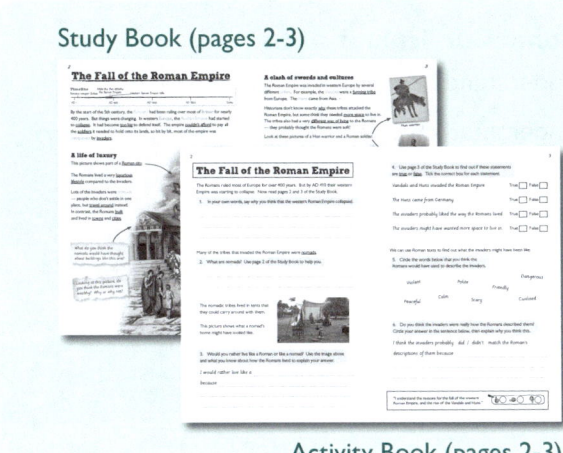

Activity Book (pages 2-3)

National Curriculum Aims

- Understand abstract terms such as 'empire'.
- Understand how empires are dissolved.
- Know about the history of the wider world.
- Understand why there are different interpretations of the past.

Introduction

As time wore on, political and economic weaknesses emerged in the Roman Empire. Attacks by nomadic tribes such as the Huns, Goths and Vandals from around AD 376 weakened it further, and contributed to its eventual downfall. As a class, discuss what pupils already know about the Romans. What are they famous for? Were they powerful? After pupils have read pages 2-3 in the Study Book, ask them whether, based on their prior knowledge of the Romans, they're surprised that the empire fell or if they think it was inevitable?

Answers to Activity Book Questions

1. E.g. The western Roman Empire collapsed because it had grown so big that it could not afford to pay the soldiers it needed to defend itself from invaders.
2. E.g. Nomads are people who don't settle in one place but travel around instead.
3. Pupils may answer either way, as long as they give a sensible reason to support their answer.
4. True — False — False — True
5. Pupils should have circled: violent / scary / dangerous.
6. Pupils may choose either option, as long as they give a sensible reason to support their choice. Pupils might comment on the fact that the Romans were biased against the invaders.

Extra Activities

- Ask pupils to imagine they are a member of a nomadic tribe invading the Roman Empire. Get them to write a diary entry detailing what they think of Rome and the Romans. How would they describe the Romans? What did they think when they saw Rome for the first time? Would they want to live there?

- Ask pupils to look at the images on page 2 in the Activity Book and the Study Book. As a class, discuss the similarities and differences between the way the Romans lived, the way the nomads lived and the way we live today. Ask pupils whether they think their lives are more like the lives of the Romans or the nomads.

- Ask pupils to write a monologue from the perspective of a Roman whose city has been attacked by invaders. How do they feel? What were the invaders like? Encourage pupils to think about how the Romans regarded the invaders. Ask volunteers to perform their monologues for the rest of the class.

- Ask pupils to look back at the drawing of Attila on page 3 in the Study Book. Remind pupils that the Romans had a negative opinion of Attila, while the Huns would have viewed him positively. Ask pupils to draw their own picture of Attila, with half the class drawing from the perspective of a Roman and the other half from the perspective of a Hun. Collect the drawings and show them to the class. Ask pupils to guess whether each drawing was done from a Roman or a Hun perspective and to explain how they can tell.

Discover & Learn British History — Anglo-Saxons

The Romans Leave Britain

Study Book (pages 4-5)

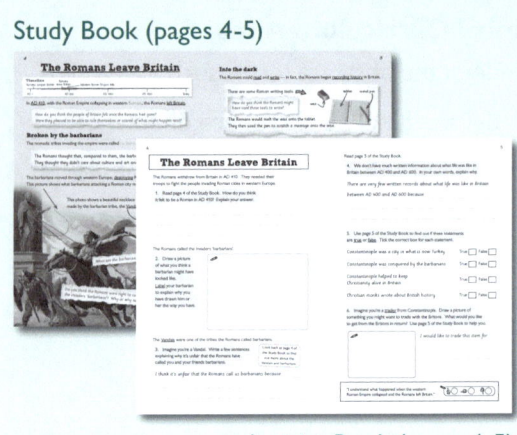

Activity Book (pages 4-5)

National Curriculum Aims
- Understand how empires are dissolved.
- Understand change.
- Understand how Britain has been influenced by the wider world.
- Understand how evidence is used to make historical claims.

Introduction

With the Roman Empire collapsing in western Europe, it wasn't long before the Romans withdrew from Britain. The Romans had had a significant impact on Britain, but much of the culture they brought with them, including the keeping of historical records, would now largely disappear. After pupils have read pages 4-5 in the Study Book, encourage them to think about why the lack of written records between AD 400 and AD 600 is significant for historians. Ask pupils to imagine that historians in the future are looking back at our society today. What else would they be able to use to find out about our lives and culture if all written records had been destroyed? Would these sources give a complete picture of life in modern Britain?

Answers to Activity Book Questions

1. Any appropriate answer. Pupils might comment on how scary it would have been to be a Roman during this time because of the barbarian attacks.
2. Any appropriate drawing. Pupils should use labels to explain why their picture looks the way it does.
3. Any appropriate answer. Pupils might comment on the fact that the Vandals were skilled craftsmen and had a culture.
4. E.g. *There are very few written records about what life was like in Britain between AD 400 and AD 600 because* the tribes that invaded the Roman Empire in this period didn't keep historical records.
5. True — False — True — True
6. Any appropriate drawing. *I would like to trade this item for* tin.

Extra Activities

- Split pupils into pairs with one pupil in each pair taking on the role of an interviewer and the other a Celtic person. Get the pupils to act out an interview about the departure of the Romans from Britain. Pupils could then swap roles and repeat the exercise, trying to come up with different questions and answers.

- Introduce pupils to the term 'stereotype'. Explain that the Romans' belief that the nomadic tribes were barbarians was a stereotype. Can pupils think of any modern stereotypes? As a class, discuss why stereotypes can be harmful.

- Give each pupil different classroom items, e.g. pens, pencils and paper clips, then ask pupils to trade their items with each other. After 10 minutes, stop the activity and see who has been the most successful trader. As a class, discuss how the bartering process worked. How did pupils work out the value of different items? Which items were seen as the most and the least valuable?

Writing About Britain

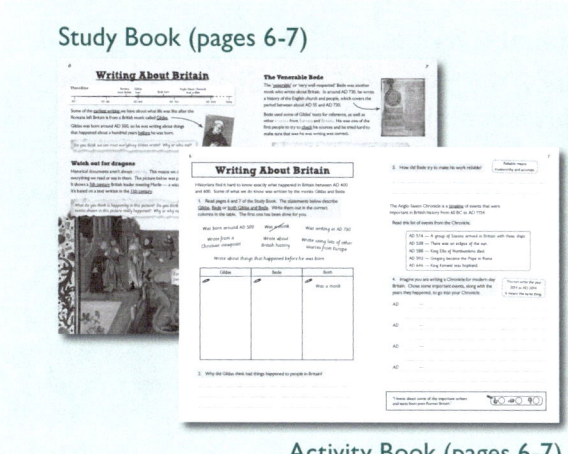

Study Book (pages 6-7)

Activity Book (pages 6-7)

National Curriculum Aims

- Understand the methods of historical enquiry.
- Understand how evidence is used to make historical claims.
- Create structured accounts.

Introduction

Pupils have already learnt about why we lack sources from post-Roman Britain. This topic will give them a chance to explore the sources that historians do have and to assess their reliability. Once pupils have read pages 6-7 in the Study Book, discuss the sorts of questions that historians need to ask themselves when evaluating a historical source (e.g. Who wrote it? Were they writing a long time after the event? Where did they get their information from? Were they writing from a particular point of view?) You could then write a list of different sources on the board (e.g. newspaper articles, diary entries, interviews, history textbooks) and ask pupils to evaluate their reliability. Which source would pupils trust the most overall? Why?

Answers to Activity Book Questions

1. *Gildas*: Was born around AD 500
   Bede: Was writing in AD 730 / Wrote using lots of other sources from Europe
   Both: Wrote from a Christian viewpoint / Wrote about British history / Wrote about things that happened before he was born

2. E.g. He thought the Britons were being punished by God for the bad things that they had done.

3. E.g. Bede tried to base his work on lots of different sources and check the sources that he used.

4. Pupils should record events that are relevant to Britain and try to give the correct years.

Extra Activities

- Ask pupils to look back at the drawing at the bottom of page 6 in the Study Book. Discuss what someone might conclude about life in fifth century Britain if they did not evaluate the picture critically. Then get pupils to draw a modern scene which includes fictional or legendary elements. As a class, discuss how someone interpreting the pupils' drawings might reach the wrong conclusions about life in Britain.

- As a class, discuss the differences between history and legend. Do pupils think legends can be useful to historians? Split the class into pairs. One pupil in each pair should write a reliable historical account of something that has happened locally and the other should write about the same event in the form of a legend. Get pupils to share their work with their partner and discuss the reliability of what they have both written and how useful it would be to a historian studying the event.

- Give pupils an event or news story from modern Britain to research. They should look at lots of different sources (e.g. articles from different news outlets, video clips) and then put together their own account of the event. As a class, compare pupils' accounts to see how they differ.

Life After the Romans

Study Book (pages 8-9)

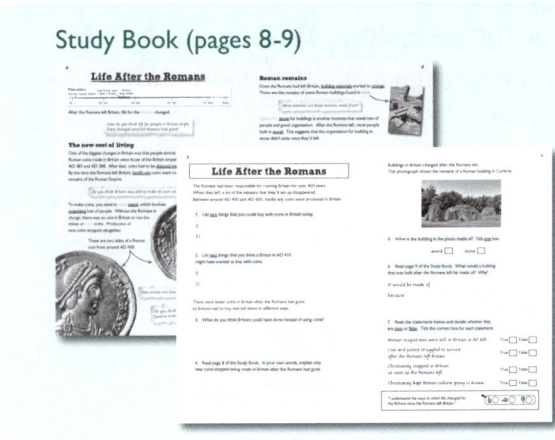

Activity Book (pages 8-9)

National Curriculum Aims
- Know the history of Britain as a chronological narrative.
- Understand similarity and difference and use them to draw contrasts.
- Understand change.

Introduction

When the Roman army withdrew in AD 410, the people of Britain were left to defend themselves; but defence wasn't the only area in which Britons would notice the Romans' absence. Because the Romans had played such a vital organisational role in areas including the economy, industry, law and religion, many of these aspects of society broke down when they left. After pupils have read pages 8-9 in the Study Book, ask the class to discuss how they think life would change if the powers that govern society today suddenly disappeared. Do they think things would change quickly? How might their daily lives be affected? What would be the most significant differences?

Answers to Activity Book Questions

1. E.g. sweets / clothes / cinema tickets / toys / books / music / magazines
2. E.g. food / material to make clothes / land / farming tools / animals / jewellery
3. E.g. Instead of using coins, I think the Britons could have traded different items with each other.
4. E.g. New coins stopped being made in Britain after the Romans had gone because there was no one left in Britain who was able to run the mines and make coins.
5. Pupils should have ticked: stone.
6. E.g. *It would be made of* wood *because* the people in Britain were not organised enough to quarry the stones needed to build stone buildings.
7. False — True — False — True

Extra Activities

- Split the class in half and hold a debate about whether life in Britain would have been better or worse after the Romans left. Encourage pupils to draw on everything they know about how the Romans changed Britain (e.g. building towns and roads, the role of the Roman army), and make sure they think about both the short- and long-term implications of the Romans' departure.

- Ask pupils to write a newspaper article with the headline "Romans Leave: Britain Steps Back in Time?" Encourage them to write a balanced argument. They could include 'quotes' they have made up from people who might have had contrasting views on the Romans' departure from Britain e.g. a magistrate, a trader.

- As a class, discuss why more ruins of stone buildings than wooden buildings survive. Ask the class to think about how this might affect our understanding of life in Britain after the departure of the Romans.

The First Invasions

Study Book (pages 10-11)

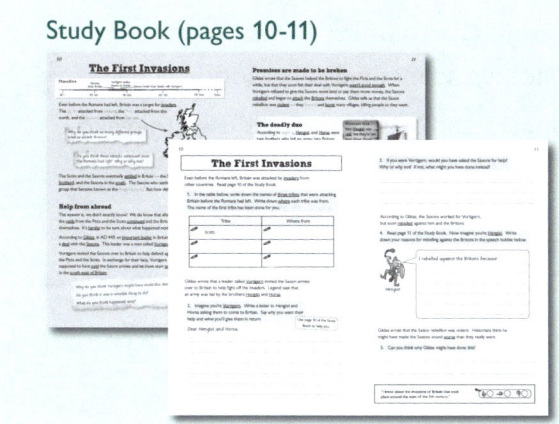

Activity Book (pages 10-11)

National Curriculum Aims

- Know the history of Britain as a chronological narrative.
- Understand cause and consequence.
- Create written narratives and structured accounts.
- Understand why there are different interpretations of the past.

Introduction

After AD 410, the people of Britain lost the protection of the Roman army, leaving them vulnerable to invasion by tribes like the Scots and the Picts. Struggling to defend themselves, it seems that leaders in Britain persuaded the Saxons, a tribe from what is now the Netherlands and northern Germany, to help them fight the invaders in return for money and land. However, the Saxons soon rebelled. According to Gildas, who lived at a time when the Anglo-Saxons controlled large areas of Britain and who deeply resented their presence, this Saxon rebellion was treacherous and violent. Bede, who completed his work about two centuries after Gildas, also described the Saxon rebellion as brutal and savage. However, Bede saw the rebellion as God's will and a punishment for immoral behaviour in Britain. Once pupils have read pages 10-11 in the Study Book, ask them what impression they have of the Saxons. Were they right to rebel against the Britons?

Answers to Activity Book Questions

1. *Scots* — Ireland / *Picts* — north Britain / *Saxons* — Europe
2. Pupils should mention needing help to fight the Picts and the Scots, and should offer money and land in the south-east of Britain in return.
3. Pupils may answer either way, as long as they give a sensible reason to support their answer.
4. E.g. *I rebelled against the Britons because* they were weak and cowardly. I knew we could defeat them easily in battle. I didn't like it when Vortigern refused to give us more land for helping him, so I decided to take land for myself.
5. E.g. I think Gildas might have done this because he didn't like the Saxons / he was angry with the Saxons.

Extra Activities

- Ask pupils to share the letters they wrote for question 2 in the Activity Book and discuss whether they think Hengist and Horsa would have found them persuasive. As a class, discuss techniques that can make writing more persuasive, such as emotive language, lists of three and repetition. Then, ask pupils to use these techniques to make an advert asking other warriors to help Vortigern.

- Get pupils to look back at the painting on page 11 in the Study Book. Ask pupils to write a short story based on the scene in the painting. What is happening? How are the Saxons arriving on the boats feeling? What are the Britons thinking and feeling? What happens when the Saxons reach the shore?

- Split pupils into groups and ask them to create and perform a play about how the Saxons came to Britain. Pupils could take on the roles of Vortigern, Hengist, Horsa and the Saxon armies.

Discover & Learn British History — Anglo-Saxons

Britain Fights Back

Study Book (pages 12-13)

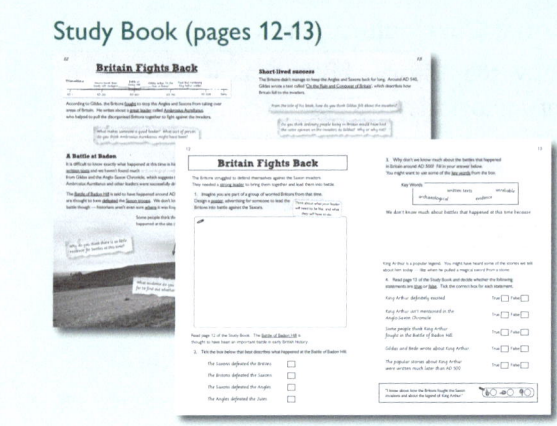

Activity Book (pages 12-13)

National Curriculum Aims

- Understand methods of historical enquiry.
- Understand how evidence is used to make historical claims.
- Understand why there are different interpretations of the past.

Introduction

The sources relating to this period of conflict in Britain are confusing, contradictory and difficult to interpret. As a result, there has been much historical debate over the existence of certain figures, especially King Arthur. Early sources, such as Gildas and Bede, do not mention Arthur at all. He first appears in the ninth-century *Historia Brittonum*, which depicts him as the leader of the British forces at the Battle of Badon Hill. In light of this, some historians argue that King Arthur is just a legend, created to serve the political purposes of the author of the *Historia Brittonum*. However, others believe that the legends have some basis in fact, pointing towards the similar achievements attributed to King Arthur and Ambrosius Aurelianus by different sources to suggest that the two names may refer to the same historical figure. Once the class has read pages 12-13 in the Study Book, hold a discussion about whether pupils think King Arthur really existed. What makes them think this?

Answers to Activity Book Questions

1. Pupils should recognise that the poster is an advert and should have used persuasive writing while making it as bright and eye-catching as possible.
2. Pupils should have ticked: The Britons defeated the Saxons.
3. E.g. *We don't know much about battles that happened at this time because* there aren't many written texts about this period and the texts may be unreliable. There's not much archaeological evidence either.
4. False — True — True — False — True

Extra Activities

- Ask pupils to imagine that they are the leader of the Britons on the eve of the Battle of Badon Hill. Get them to write a speech rallying their men for the fight against the Saxons.

- As a class, discuss how we know about wars, battles and other events that take place today (e.g. newspapers, television reports and social media). Ask pupils to write a report of the Battle of Badon Hill in the style of one of these modern news sources.

- The legend of King Arthur is still told in modern times. Ask pupils to research how Arthur is portrayed today in television, films and books. Is he always portrayed as a hero? Are there common recurring traits or features? Why do pupils think there are so many adaptations of the Arthurian legend?

- Ask pupils to write their own legend set in early sixth-century Britain featuring a heroic figure. Get them to think about whether their hero is a Briton or a Saxon, and what their legendary feat will be.

Becoming Anglo-Saxon

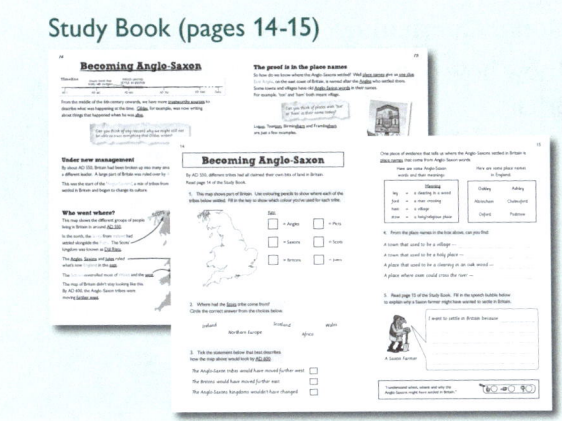

Study Book (pages 14-15)

Activity Book (pages 14-15)

National Curriculum Aims

- Know the history of Britain as a chronological narrative.
- Understand how Britain has been influenced by the wider world.
- Understand the connections between local and national history.
- Understand change.

Introduction

Despite the Britons' efforts to resist the invading European tribes in the early sixth century, by AD 550 the invaders controlled a large part of eastern England, and over the following decades they continued to expand further west. As they expanded, the invaders established settlements and gave them Anglo-Saxon names. This place-name evidence is a valuable source of information for historians investigating the extent of Anglo-Saxon settlement in Britain. Many places were named for a local tribal leader. For example, Hastings, known to the Anglo-Saxons as Haestingas, is thought to have been named after a leader called Haesta. The suffix 'ingas' can mean 'the people', so Hastings translates as 'The people of Haesta'. After reading pages 14-15 in the Study Book, ask pupils what country they would like to move to and why. How easy do they think it would be to build a new village in a foreign country today?

Answers to Activity Book Questions

1. The borders of each tribe's territory should match the map on page 14 in the Study Book. The key should be correctly colour coded to match the areas where each tribe settled.
2. Pupils should have circled: Ireland.
3. Pupils should have ticked: The Anglo-Saxon tribes would have moved further west.
4. Altrincham, Padstow, Oakley, Oxford
5. E.g. *I want to settle in Britain because* the area where I live is very bad for farming. It always floods! Britain has very fertile land so it is perfect for farming and growing crops.

Extra Activities

- Using the map on page 14 in the Study Book, get pupils to find out which tribe was in control of their area in AD 550. Pupils could then find the names of towns, cities or villages near them and research the origins of these place names. What does each name mean? Do any of them have Anglo-Saxon origins?

- Get pupils to research where the Angles, Saxons and Jutes originally came from. They should shade these areas on a map and label them. What countries would these areas be in today?

- Ask pupils to imagine that they are part of a Romano-British family living in a small village. A group of Saxons settle nearby. One day, a Saxon man comes seeking the services of the pupils' healing woman as his son is ill. Some people in the village think the woman shouldn't help them. Get pupils to write a speech explaining to the people in their village why they think it's a good idea to be friendly to the newcomers.

Anglo-Saxon Settlements

Study Book (pages 16-17)

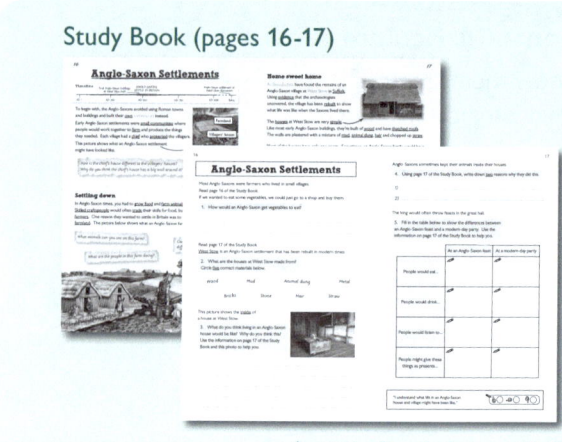

Activity Book (pages 16-17)

National Curriculum Aims

- Know how people's lives have shaped Britain.
- Understand similarity and difference and use them to draw contrasts.

Introduction

Instead of moving into abandoned Roman settlements, the early Anglo-Saxons chose to build their own villages and let Roman buildings fall into decay. Anglo-Saxon villages were very different to Roman towns — they were usually small, being inhabited by only a few families, and the houses were made of wood instead of stone. The Anglo-Saxons chose land which was well suited to their livestock and crops, and made sure their settlements were near natural resources such as woodland and rivers. This enabled the new communities to be largely self-sufficient, so there was little trade between villages. Although the Anglo-Saxons didn't build impressive stone buildings comparable with Roman villas, they did build large timber halls where their kings lived and entertained. After pupils have read pages 16-17 in the Study Book, ask them why they think the early Anglo-Saxons built their own houses and villages rather than using Roman settlements.

Answers to Activity Book Questions

1. E.g. They would grow their own vegetables or trade their skills for them.
2. Pupils should have circled: Wood / Mud / Animal dung / Hair / Straw.
3. Any appropriate answer. Pupils should use information from the Study Book and the photograph to support their answer.
4. E.g. To help to keep the house warm. / To keep the animals safe from wolves and bears.
5. E.g. *Anglo-Saxon feast*: *Eat* — roast meats / *Drink* — mead or beer / *Listen to* — stories or music played on a lyre / *Presents* — jewellery or treasure
   Modern-day party: *Eat* — crisps or cake / *Drink* — cola or lemonade / *Listen to* — pop music / *Presents* — toys or clothes

Extra Activities

- Ask pupils to imagine they have travelled back to Anglo-Saxon times and are living in an Anglo-Saxon settlement. Get them to write a story based on their experiences. How do they feel about living in the same house as farm animals? How do they cope without modern comforts? Pupils might write about sneaking into the great hall of an Anglo-Saxon king. What do they see and hear in the hall?

- Get pupils to look at the picture of the house from West Stow on page 17 in the Study Book. Ask pupils to draw their home and compare it to the house from West Stow. Get them to label their picture with similarities and differences in building materials, structure, lighting, etc.

- Ask pupils to write a poem to be recited at an Anglo-Saxon feast. It could describe what life was like in an Anglo-Saxon village or recount the tale of one of the figures the pupils have learnt about so far.

Daily Life for Anglo-Saxons

Study Book (pages 18-19)

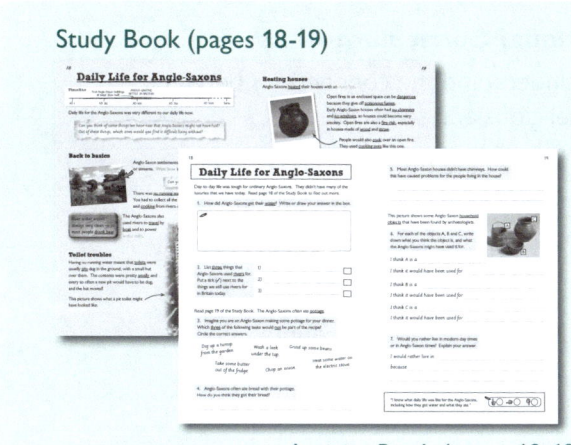

Activity Book (pages 18-19)

National Curriculum Aims

- Know how people's lives have shaped Britain.
- Understand similarity and difference and use them to draw contrasts.

Introduction

For the average Anglo-Saxon, life was all about survival: farming for food, fighting in battles and maintaining their living spaces. Although there wasn't much time for leisure activities, the Anglo-Saxons enjoyed creating riddles and playing dice games and board games, such as Nine Men's Morris. Before the class reads pages 18-19 in the Study Book, find some Anglo-Saxon riddles and see if pupils can solve them. What do they think of this as a pastime compared to their modern hobbies? Once pupils have read pages 18-19 in the Study Book, ask them to identify the major differences between daily life in the Anglo-Saxon period and in the modern day.

Answers to Activity Book Questions

1. E.g. If an Anglo-Saxon wanted water, they would have had to go and collect it from a nearby river, stream or well. Pupils may have given their answer as a drawing.
2. E.g. Water for washing and cooking (unticked) / Travelling by boat (ticked) / Powering water mills (ticked)
3. Pupils should have circled: Wash a leek under the tap. / Take some butter out of the fridge. / Heat some water on the electric stove.
4. E.g. I think they baked it themselves.
5. E.g. It made the house smoky. / It meant that poisonous gases from the fire couldn't escape.
6. Any sensible suggestions. E.g. A is a bucket, used for carrying water / beer. B is a bowl, used for eating from. C is a jar / cooking pot, used for storing food / cooking.
7. Pupils may answer either way, as long as they give a sensible reason to support their answer.

Extra Activities

- Split pupils into groups to create a short play to show what a day might have been like for ordinary Anglo-Saxons. Encourage them to cover at least three aspects of their daily routine.
- Find a recipe for pottage on the internet and make some with the class in a cookery lesson. Have pupils ever eaten anything similar before? Do they like it? Would they be happy to eat it on a daily basis?
- Get pupils to keep a food diary for a day and then have them compare the food they eat with the sorts of foods that an Anglo-Saxon would have eaten. Discuss how and why the foods they eat are different.
- Ask pupils to imagine they are a village chief. They have decided to throw a feast to reward the villagers for working hard. Ask pupils to create a poster advertising the feast. Where will it be held? What games and fun things will there be to do? What food will be served?

Discover & Learn British History — Anglo-Saxons

Anglo-Saxon Religions

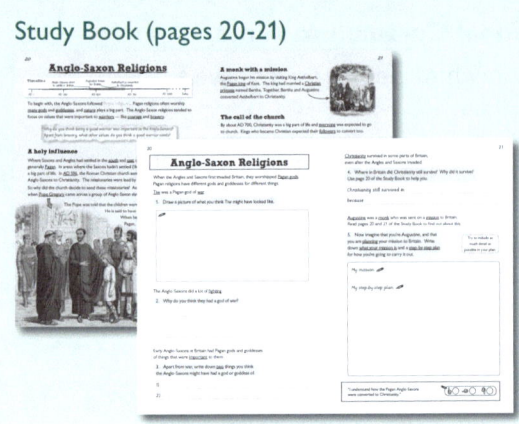

Study Book (pages 20-21)

Activity Book (pages 20-21)

National Curriculum Aims

- Understand the connections between religious and social history.
- Understand how Britain has been influenced by the wider world.
- Know the history of Britain as a chronological narrative.
- Create structured accounts.

Introduction

The Romans had brought Christianity to Britain in the fourth century, but the invading Germanic tribes were Pagans and continued to practise their religion when they settled in Britain. Although Christianity survived in areas such as Wales, by the sixth century Anglo-Saxon England was predominantly Pagan. The first concerted effort to convert the Anglo-Saxons to Christianity came with Augustine's successful mission to King Aethelbert of Kent in AD 596. Over the following decades, further missions gradually persuaded other Anglo-Saxon rulers to adopt Christianity. These missions were often sponsored by Anglo-Saxon kings who had already converted, although they sometimes involved external missionaries from either mainland Europe or Ireland. The conversion process was not straightforward, because some Anglo-Saxon kingdoms reverted to Paganism after the death of a converted ruler. Nonetheless, by the late 680s, less than 90 years after Augustine's initial mission, the whole of Anglo-Saxon England had adopted Christianity.

Answers to Activity Book Questions

1. Any appropriate drawing. Tiw is often drawn as a strong man with a large sword and shield.
2. E.g. I think the Anglo-Saxons had a god of war because fighting and winning battles were very important to them. They thought their god of war would help them win battles.
3. E.g. farming / wealth
4. *Christianity still survived in* Wales *because* the Anglo-Saxons had not settled there.
5. E.g. *My mission:* Convert the Anglo-Saxons to Christianity. *My step-by-step plan:* Travel to Kent. / Visit King Aethelbert of Kent, who is a Pagan. / Speak to the king's wife, Bertha, who is a Christian. / Get Bertha's help to convert Aethelbert to Christianity.

Extra Activities

- Explain to pupils that the Pagan gods Tiw, Woden, Thunor and Frige gave their names to four days of the week — Tuesday, Wednesday, Thursday and Friday. Split the class into groups and get them to research one of the latter three gods. What were they the god of? Why do pupils think they were important to the Anglo-Saxons? Are they still known today, possibly in other forms through television or other media? Pupils should present their findings to the class.
- Ask pupils to look at the drawing on page 20 in the Study Book and write a short story based on this scene, ending with Pope Gregory vowing to send missionaries to Britain.
- Ask pupils to research the life of Augustine of Canterbury and write a biography of him. When was he born? Where did he live before he was sent to Britain? What were his main achievements while in Britain?

Anglo-Saxon Law

Study Book (pages 22-23)

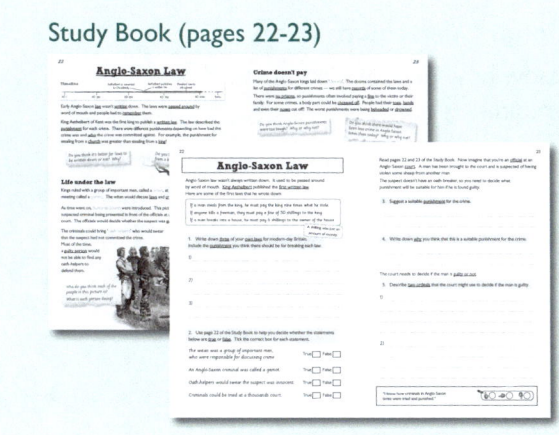

Activity Book (pages 22-23)

National Curriculum Aims

- Create structured accounts.
- Understand the achievements and follies of mankind.
- Understand change.

Introduction

Because the Anglo-Saxons didn't initially keep written records, information about their early legal system is extremely limited. However, the resurgence of Christianity from the seventh century onwards brought literacy back to Anglo-Saxon England and established written documents as important status symbols that were highly valued by rulers. As a result, Anglo-Saxon kings began to issue written law codes, the earliest of which is that of King Aethelbert, issued after his conversion in c. AD 600. The rise of Christianity in England was also reflected in the content of these law codes, which included fines for those stealing from the Church and measures to enforce religious practices such as baptism. Once pupils have read pages 22-23 in the Study Book, ask them if they think it is important for laws to be written down. Why do they think this?

Answers to Activity Book Questions

1. Any appropriate answers. E.g. If you steal something from a shop, you should pay the shopkeeper twice what the object you stole was worth.
2. True — False — True — False
3. E.g. He should have to pay a fine. / He should have a body part chopped off. / He should be drowned or beheaded.
4. Any appropriate answer. Pupils may link their punishment to how severe they think the crime is.
5. Pupils should describe the trials by water and hot water, explaining how each trial would show if the suspect was innocent or guilty.

Extra Activities

- Explain to pupils that the fine for killing or harming a person was called wergild. Without wergild, victims of crime and their families retaliated against the perpetrator, leading to further retaliation and a cycle of violence known as a blood feud. Sometimes whole families were killed in blood feuds. Ask pupils to write a leaflet persuading Anglo-Saxons that paying wergild is a better system than fighting blood feuds.

- Have pupils re-enact an Anglo-Saxon court case where a suspected thief is being tried for stealing an animal or food. Get pupils to take on the roles of officials, the suspect, the victim and oath-helpers.

- Ask pupils to discuss how and why the punishments for crimes today are different to Anglo-Saxon punishments. They could also discuss why crimes need to be punished and whether they think Anglo-Saxon or modern punishments work better.

Discover & Learn British History — Anglo-Saxons

The Top of Society

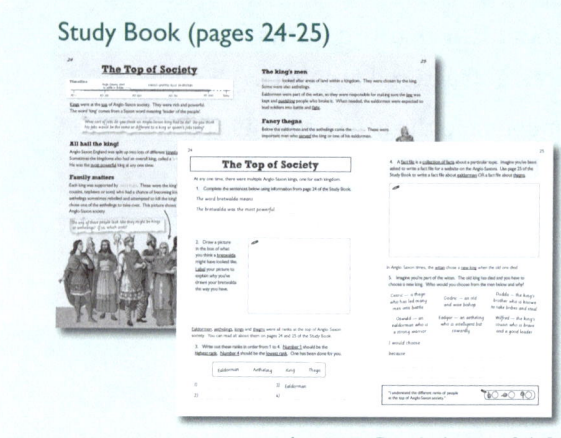

Study Book (pages 24-25)

Activity Book (pages 24-25)

National Curriculum Aims

- Know how people's lives have shaped Britain.
- Understand the connections between social and political history.
- Create structured accounts.

Introduction

Although kings were at the top of the Anglo-Saxon social hierarchy, this didn't grant them immunity from the violence of the period. Whether it was due to war or the plotting of other noblemen, kings struggled to stay alive. The kingdom of Wessex, for example, had ten different rulers in the seventh century. Kings were supported (and occasionally assassinated) by ealdormen who combined legislative and military roles, sitting on the witan and acting as war leaders. Lesser members of the elite, known as thegns, were military men with their own land. Although social mobility was limited in Anglo-Saxon England, thegns were occasionally able to rise to the level of ealdorman. Once pupils have read pages 24-25 in the Study Book, ask them to discuss whether they would rather be an Anglo-Saxon king or a modern-day monarch.

Answers to Activity Book Questions

1. *The word bretwalda means* Britain-ruler. *The bretwalda was the most powerful* king in Britain at any one time.

2. Any appropriate drawing. Pupils should show that bretwaldas were wealthy and powerful.

3. 1) King 2) Aetheling 3) *Ealdorman* 4) Thegn

4. E.g. Ealdormen looked after areas of land in a kingdom. They were chosen by the king. They could be aethelings. They were part of the witan. OR E.g. Thegns were military men. They served the king or an ealdorman. They acted as soldiers or bodyguards. They were given their own land in payment.

5. Any appropriate answer. Pupils should support their choice with a sensible reason.

Extra Activities

- Ask pupils to use the information on pages 24-25 in the Study Book to draw the Anglo-Saxon social hierarchy. They should draw each person (king, aetheling, ealdorman, thegn) in order of their importance and label them. Once pupils have read pages 28-29, they could add ceorls and slaves to their drawings.

- Ask pupils to write a job advert for the role of king of Wessex. Encourage them to think about the tasks the king had to carry out and the skills someone would need to do the job successfully.

- As a class, discuss how Anglo-Saxon kings were chosen. How do we decide on the leader of the country today? What is the difference between how the monarch and the Prime Minister are chosen? You could hold a class debate about which of the three systems is the best way to choose a leader.

- As a class, discuss why Anglo-Saxon kings needed the support of aethelings and ealdormen. Who might be the equivalent of such people today (e.g. politicians, policemen, judges)? What roles do they play in our society? Do their roles differ from those played by their Anglo-Saxon counterparts?

Beowulf and Sutton Hoo

Study Book (pages 26-27)

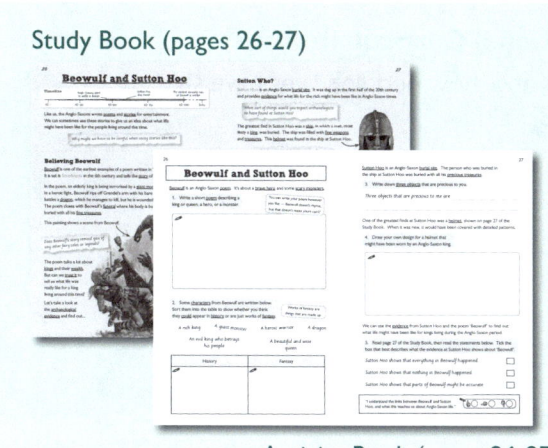

Activity Book (pages 26-27)

National Curriculum Aims
- Create written narratives.
- Understand methods of historical enquiry.
- Understand how evidence is used to make historical claims.

Introduction

Although Beowulf is set in sixth-century Scandinavia, it is thought to have been written in Anglo-Saxon England. The only surviving manuscript dates from c. AD 1000, but there is much debate about whether the poem itself was composed around this time or centuries earlier. Because the poem includes mythical elements like dragons and monsters, historians traditionally regarded it as a work of fiction. However, the archaeological findings at Sutton Hoo seem to confirm many of the aspects of Anglo-Saxon society and culture described in Beowulf, and this has persuaded historians to take the poem more seriously. Once pupils have read pages 26-27 in the Study Book, ask them why they think historians might have regarded Beowulf as an unreliable source. Discuss the challenges of distinguishing between fact and fiction in historical sources. To aid a greater understanding of Beowulf, it might be helpful to read the class an extract from a simplified translation of the poem.

Answers to Activity Book Questions

1. E.g. A dragon lived inside a cave, / He guarded lots of treasure. / The shiny coins and jewels he owned, / He counted at his leisure. / His teeth were sharp, his claws were long, / His scales were strong as steel. / And no one would dare wake him up, / Or they'd become his meal!

2. *History*: a heroic warrior / an evil king who betrays his people / a beautiful and wise queen / a rich king
   Fantasy: a giant monster / a dragon

3. E.g. *Three objects that are precious to me are* my bike / my photographs / my computer.

4. Any appropriate drawing of a helmet.

5. Pupils should have ticked: Sutton Hoo shows that parts of Beowulf might be accurate.

Extra Activities

- Ask pupils to think of some stories that are set in modern day Britain. These could be from books, films or TV programmes. For each story, ask them to list aspects of the story that could be real and aspects that could only be works of fantasy.

- Ask pupils to research the treasures that were found at Sutton Hoo and make a model of one of them, using papier-mâché or card, paint and tin foil.

- Ask pupils to draw a storyboard for Beowulf using information from page 26 in the Study Book and the extract you read to them. Get them to think about the best way of splitting the story into different frames.

- Make sure pupils understand what alliteration is, and explain that it was used a lot in Anglo-Saxon poetry. Ask pupils to write a second verse to the poem they wrote for question 1 in the Activity Book, using alliteration in every line. Ask for volunteers to read their poems aloud to the class.

The Bottom of Society

Study Book (pages 28-29)

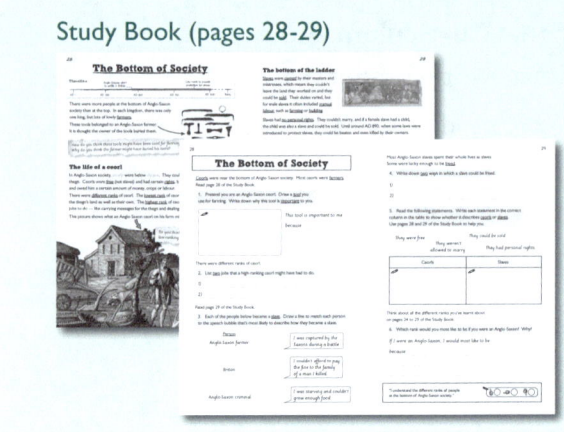

Activity Book (pages 28-29)

National Curriculum Aims
- Know how people's lives have shaped Britain.
- Understand similarity and difference.

Introduction

The boundaries between Anglo-Saxon social groups were not always clear cut. For example, although ceorls were of lower social status than thegns, some wealthy ceorls probably owned more land than the poorest thegns. There was also scope for mobility between the different social groups. Anglo-Saxon law codes suggest that ceorls could become thegns if they met certain conditions, and slaves occasionally gained their freedom. Equally, members of higher social groups could lose their status and be forced into slavery as a punishment for committing certain crimes. Once pupils have read pages 28-29 in the Study Book, ask them to think back to what they have already learnt about the top of Anglo-Saxon society (pages 24-25 in the Study Book). How would life have been different for people at the bottom of society compared to those at the top?

Answers to Activity Book Questions

1. E.g. A picture of a scythe blade. *This tool is important to me because* it allows me to grow food for my family.

2. E.g. Carry messages / Deal with visitors to his master's house

3. Anglo-Saxon farmer — I was starving and couldn't grow enough food.
   Briton — I was captured by the Saxons during a battle.
   Anglo-Saxon criminal — I couldn't afford to pay the fine to the family of a man I killed.

4. E.g. They could buy their freedom. / They could be set free when their masters died.

5. *Ceorls*: They were free. / They had personal rights.
   Slaves: They weren't allowed to marry. / They could be sold.

6. Any appropriate answer. Pupils should support their choice with a sensible reason.

Extra Activities

- As a class, discuss whether slaves were as important to Anglo-Saxon society as people of higher social status. What might Anglo-Saxon England have been like without a king, without thegns or without slaves?

- Get pupils to imagine they are a ceorl and to write a diary entry about a day in their life. Are they high- or low-ranking? What sort of work do they do? Do they wish they could change their rank?

- Ask pupils to imagine they are slaves whose master has died and set them free. In pairs, ask them to act out a conversation they might have the night before their release. How do they feel about their future? Do they think life will be better for them once they're free?

- Split pupils into groups and ask them to act out a short scene featuring members of the different Anglo-Saxon social groups: ruler, ealdormen, thegns, ceorls and slaves. Make sure they highlight the differences between each group. To what extent do they think the groups would have interacted with one another?

Anglo-Saxon Women

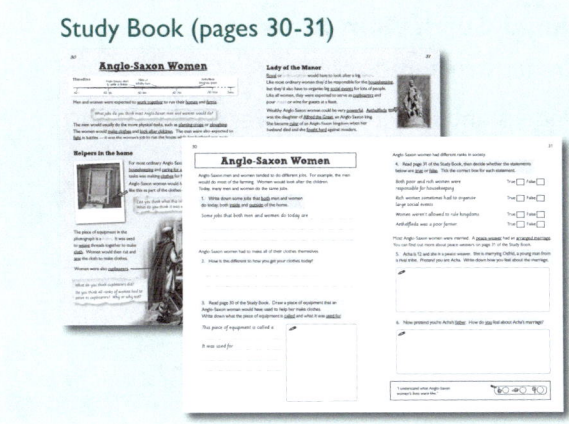

Study Book (pages 30-31)

Activity Book (pages 30-31)

National Curriculum Aims

- Understand how people's lives have shaped Britain.
- Understand similarity and difference and use them to draw contrasts.
- Understand change.
- Create written narratives.

Introduction

Although men and women weren't equal in Anglo-Saxon society, Anglo-Saxon women had more rights and freedom than women of many other historical periods. When women married, they received a gift from their husband, known as morgengifu. This took the form of money or land, and was under the woman's personal control — she could sell or bequeath it without consulting her husband. According to one of King Aethelbert's laws, women were also free to leave a marriage, and if they did so, they were entitled to take any children and half of the couple's shared property. However, divorce seems to have been relatively rare. After reading pages 30-31 in the Study Book, ask pupils to discuss the similarities and differences between the lives of Anglo-Saxon women and women living in Britain today.

Answers to Activity Book Questions

1. E.g. *Some jobs that both men and women do today are* cleaning / cooking / ironing / hoovering / doctors / shop keepers / politicians / electricians / bus drivers.

2. E.g. Today I don't have to make my own clothes. I can go and buy them from a shop.

3. Pupils should have drawn a loom. E.g. *This piece of equipment is called a* loom. *It was used for* weaving threads together to make cloth.

4. True — True — False — False

5. Any appropriate answer.

6. Any appropriate answer. Pupils may recognise that Acha and her father might have different views.

Extra Activities

- Ask pupils to write a diary entry describing a day in the life of an Anglo-Saxon woman. They could choose to write from the perspective of an ordinary farmer's wife or a wealthy noblewoman.

- Ask pupils to discuss whether they would rather have been a man or a woman in Anglo-Saxon England. Who do they think had a more exciting life? Who do they think would have been likely to live longer? Would social status affect their choice (e.g. might it have been better to be a rich woman than a poor man)?

- Ask pupils to research Hilda of Whitby and the legend of her turning snakes into stone. Split students into small groups and ask them to perform a short scene showing their interpretation of this legend.

- Ordinary Anglo-Saxon women and girls would have worn long dresses, while men and boys usually wore a thick tunic over a pair of trousers. Richer people would have had more decorative clothes. Ask pupils to find out more about Anglo-Saxon clothes and then design an Anglo-Saxon-style outfit for themselves.

Anglo-Saxon Children

Study Book (pages 32-33)

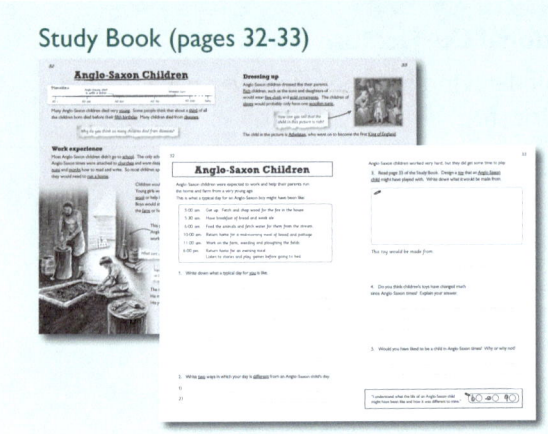

Activity Book (pages 32-33)

National Curriculum Aims
- Create structured accounts.
- Understand how people's lives have shaped Britain.
- Understand similarity and difference and use them to draw contrasts.
- Understand change.

Introduction

Anglo-Saxon life involved a lot of hard work, for children as much as for adults. Even royal children might have to take on a lot of responsibility at a young age. For example, Edward the Martyr became king of England when he was around thirteen years old. Only a small minority of children — members of wealthy families who were training to become monks or nuns — received a formal education, and this focused primarily on Latin and the study of religious texts. The majority would learn a trade or farming skills from their parents. After reading pages 32-33 in the Study Book, ask pupils how they would feel if they didn't have to go to school. Would they feel differently if the alternative was to live like an Anglo-Saxon child?

Answers to Activity Book Questions

1. Any appropriate answer. Pupils should write about a full day from their lives, including the times at which they do different activities.
2. E.g. I wake up later than Anglo-Saxon children. / I go to school instead of working on a farm.
3. E.g. A drawing of a doll made from rags or a board game made from wood and bone.
4. Pupils may answer either way, as long as they give sensible reasons to support their answer.
5. Pupils may answer either way, as long as they give a sensible reason to support their answer.

Extra Activities

- Ask pupils to make an Anglo-Saxon toy or game using twigs, wool and scraps of fabric. They could base it on their drawing for question 3 in the Activity Book or they could research other Anglo-Saxon toys.
- As a class, discuss whether pupils think Anglo-Saxon childhoods lasted as long as they do today. Encourage them to think about how long Anglo-Saxon children studied for, if at all, and the age at which they were expected to do 'grown-up' things such as housework and farming.
- Split the class in two and ask pupils to debate whether Anglo-Saxon children learnt more valuable skills than modern-day children learn at school. They should think about what both sets of children would learn and how useful their education would be for their adult lives.
- Ask pupils to think about the differences between their lives and the lives of Anglo-Saxon children. What do they think Anglo-Saxon children would find most surprising or challenging about modern life? Ask them to write a story exploring what might happen if an Anglo-Saxon child were to time travel to the present day.

The Anglo-Saxon Kingdoms

Study Book (pages 34-35)

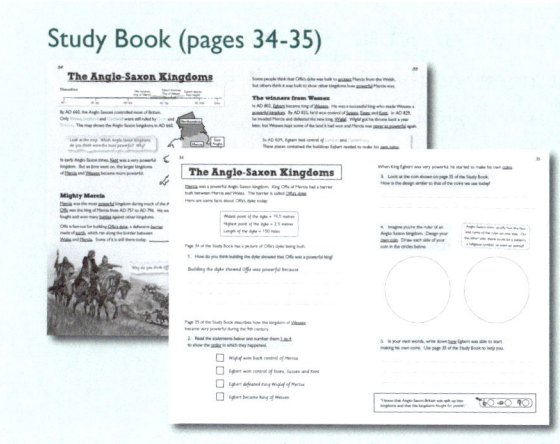

Activity Book (pages 34-35)

National Curriculum Aims

- Understand the history of Britain as a chronological narrative.
- Understand the achievements of mankind.
- Understand change.

Introduction

Although the Anglo-Saxons controlled most of England by the mid-seventh century, the country still wasn't unified, and its division into seven competing kingdoms led to almost constant warfare in the centuries that followed. King Offa of Mercia seems to have been a particularly warlike leader — as well as fighting numerous times against the Britons in Wales, his 39-year reign also saw conflicts with Kent, Sussex, East Anglia and, to a lesser extent, Wessex. Historians regard Offa as one of the most powerful Anglo-Saxon kings, but in the ninth century Wessex eventually superseded Mercia as the dominant Anglo-Saxon kingdom. Once pupils have read pages 34-35 in the Study Book, ask them to discuss which kingdom they would have liked to belong to. What are their reasons?

Answers to Activity Book Questions

1. E.g. *Building the dyke showed Offa was powerful because* the dyke must have been built by hand. Offa would have needed to be in charge of lots of people to build the dyke.

2. 1) Egbert became king of Wessex. 2) Egbert won control of Essex, Sussex and Kent. 3) Egbert defeated King Wiglaf of Mercia. 4) Wiglaf won back control of Mercia.

3. E.g. King Egbert's coin is similar to coins we use today because it is round and has the picture and name of the ruler on one side.

4. Any appropriate coin design.

5. E.g. Egbert won control of London and Canterbury by AD 829. These places had buildings where coins were made. Egbert was able to make his own coins in these buildings.

Extra Activities

- In the playground, ask pupils to measure out 19.5 metres and 2.5 metres to get a sense of how wide and high Offa's dyke is now. They could compare its length (150 miles) with how far they live from school.

- Using page 35 in the Study Book, ask pupils to create a timeline showing the events of King Egbert's reign. Encourage them to do their own research to add extra detail to the timeline. They could also draw a map to show how much of Britain was ruled by Wessex at the end of Egbert's reign.

- Ask pupils to share their answers to question 1 in the Activity Book. Do they think Offa's dyke was an effective way for Offa to demonstrate his power? Why or why not? Pupils could then imagine they are the ruler of one of the Anglo-Saxon kingdoms in AD 660 and design an object to show their power. It could be a statue of themselves, a weapon covered in expensive jewels or a new form of currency.

Discover & Learn British History — Anglo-Saxons

The Golden Age

Study Book (pages 36-37)

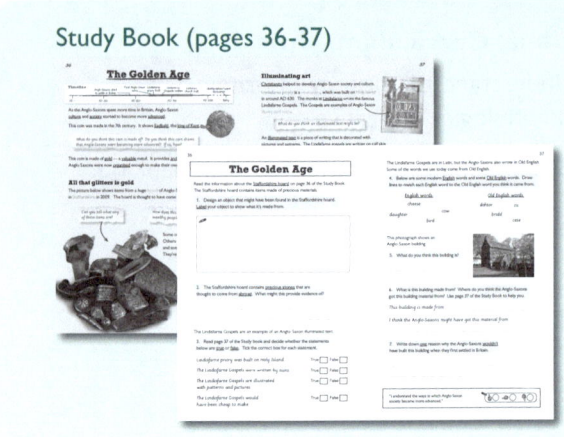

Activity Book (pages 36-37)

National Curriculum Aims

- Understand the history of Britain as a chronological narrative.
- Understand the achievements of mankind.
- Understand how evidence is used to make historical claims.
- Understand change.

Introduction

The Anglo-Saxons produced beautiful, intricate works of art in a wide range of media. They are particularly renowned for their skill as metal workers, and some of the earliest surviving works of Anglo-Saxon art are the weapons and other military items found in the Sutton Hoo ship burial and the Staffordshire Hoard. These objects, which are thought to date from the sixth and seventh centuries, are beautifully decorated with gold and precious stones. Following the Anglo-Saxons' religious conversion in the seventh century, Christianity became an important influence on Anglo-Saxon art, and monks at English monasteries began to produce manuscripts decorated with detailed, colourful and complex patterns. The Lindisfarne Gospels is perhaps the most famous of these illuminated texts, but many more survive from monasteries throughout Anglo-Saxon England.

Answers to Activity Book Questions

1. Any appropriate design. Pupils should use labels to show that the object is made of gold and precious stones.
2. E.g. It provides evidence that the Anglo-Saxons in Britain were wealthy and might have traded with foreign countries.
3. True — False — True — False
4. cheese — cese / cow — cu / daughter — dohtor / bird — bridd
5. a church
6. *This building is made from* stone. *I think the Anglo-Saxons might have got this material from* taking apart old Roman buildings and settlements.
7. E.g. When the Anglo-Saxons first arrived in Britain they built with wood not stone.

Extra Activities

- Explain to pupils that the Staffordshire Hoard can help us to understand the things rich people valued in the Anglo-Saxon period. As a class, discuss how the items in the hoard are different from the things that people spend a lot of money on today. Why might this be?
- Show pupils some pictures of the Lindisfarne Gospels and other illuminated manuscripts (e.g. the Book of Durrow, the Lichfield Gospels, the Stockholm Codex Aureus). Ask pupils to create their own illuminated text. They should copy out a short passage from one of their favourite books and then decorate it with intricate borders and a large, elaborate first letter.
- Read pupils a story and then ask them to write it down. Ask pupils to compare their versions of the story to see how similar or different they are. Then, provide pupils with a copy of your original story. Did they remember all the details? As a class, discuss the advantages and disadvantages of written and oral storytelling.

Defending Against Invaders

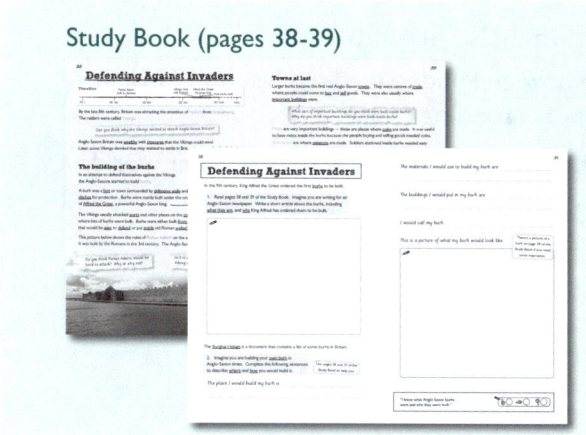

Study Book (pages 38-39)

Activity Book (pages 38-39)

National Curriculum Aims

- Understand how Britain has been influenced by the wider world.
- Understand cause and consequence.
- Understand the achievements of mankind.

Introduction

When Alfred the Great became king of Wessex in AD 871, the Vikings had already been raiding Britain for almost a century. Alfred recognised the Vikings' tactic of launching small-scale attacks on vulnerable positions and took action to counter it. He restructured the military, designed an improved naval fleet and built burhs throughout his kingdom. These fortified settlements provided people living nearby with somewhere to take refuge during a Viking raid, and Alfred aimed to ensure that no one lived more than 20 miles away from one. Once pupils have read pages 38-39 in the Study Book, ask them to discuss whether they think burhs would have been popular with the people of ninth-century England. Why or why not?

Answers to Activity Book Questions

1. Any appropriate answer. Pupils should use as much information from pages 38-39 in the Study Book as possible.

2. E.g. *The place I would build my burh is* on the coast near Hastings, in the south-east of England.
   The materials I would use to build my burh are stone and wood.
   The buildings I would put in my burh are mints and armouries.
   I would call my burh Fortisburh.
   Any appropriate drawing of a burh.

Extra Activities

- Ask pupils to write a short story from the perspective of a Viking raider approaching Britain on a longship. What do they hope to find in Britain? What can they see as they approach land? Are they successful in their raid or are they forced back?

- Ask pupils to make a leaflet that will persuade people to live in the burh they created on pages 38-39 in the Activity Book. What makes it a safe place to shelter from Viking raids? What buildings does it have that would make it a good place to live? Encourage pupils to use persuasive techniques like lists of three, rhetorical questions and emotive language.

- Remind pupils that burhs became the first real Anglo-Saxon towns. Ask them to imagine they are building a new town today. In what ways would their new town be similar to an Anglo-Saxon burh? How would it be different?

- Ask pupils to research Alfred the Great and produce an obituary. How and when did he die? What were his greatest achievements as king? Was he remembered fondly?

Discover & Learn British History — Anglo-Saxons

Who Were the Vikings?

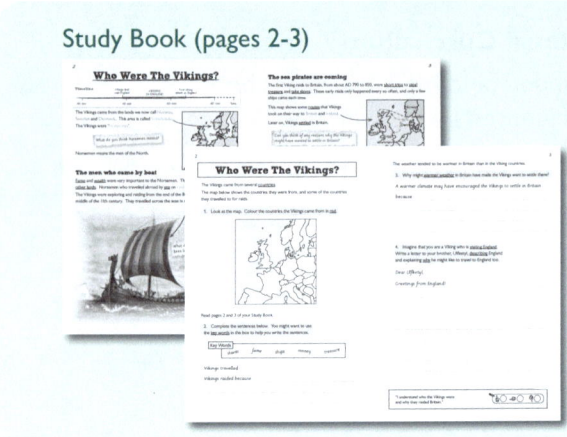

Study Book (pages 2-3)

Activity Book (pages 2-3)

National Curriculum Aims

- Know and understand the history of Britain as a chronological narrative.
- Know about the history of the wider world.
- Create structured accounts.

Introduction

The Vikings were explorers, traders, raiders and settlers. From their homelands in Scandinavia, they travelled by ship to places as far afield as Turkey, Italy and Canada. This mobility allowed them to trade all over Europe, Russia and parts of Asia, establishing trade routes and trading centres as they went. The Vikings also engaged in raids and violent attacks, with Britain's monasteries, towns and villages being among their targets. However, the Vikings came to see Britain as somewhere more than just a place to raid — those who had no land in Scandinavia, or who simply wanted more or better land, decided to settle and farm there. Before pupils read pages 2-3 in the Study Book, ask them to write down what they already know, or think they know, about the Vikings. Then discuss what they have written as a class.

Answers to Activity Book Questions

1. Pupils should have coloured in Norway, Sweden and Denmark on the map.
2. E.g. *Vikings travelled* across the sea in ships. *Vikings raided because* they wanted to make money and find fame. They did this by stealing treasure and taking people to use as slaves.
3. E.g. *A warmer climate may have encouraged the Vikings to settle in Britain because* it might have made it easier to farm. Crops would have grown better there than in the colder Viking countries. It might also have been more pleasant to live in a warmer place.
4. Pupils' letters should be written in the first person. Pupils should use as much information from pages 2-3 in the Study Book as possible, as well as their own imaginations.

Extra Activities

- Explain to pupils that, as well as Britain, the Vikings also raided other countries such as Ireland, France, Finland, Spain and Italy. Get pupils to find out where these countries are, then colour and label them on the map on page 2 in the Activity Book.

- Ask pupils to look back at the letter they wrote on page 3 in the Activity Book. Get them to research Old Norse names and their meaning, and then choose one to sign their letter off with. Pupils can then share their choice with the rest of the class. Challenge pupils to only refer to themselves and each other by their Viking names for the rest of their lessons on the Vikings.

- Get pupils to make a poster aimed at Vikings that promotes the benefits of moving to Britain. They should think carefully about their choice of language in order to make their posters as persuasive as possible.

- Ask pupils to imagine meeting a Viking for the first time. What would they notice? What would they think of them? Ask pupils to write a diary entry about the encounter.

Discover & Learn British History — Vikings

Viking Values

Study Book (pages 4-5)

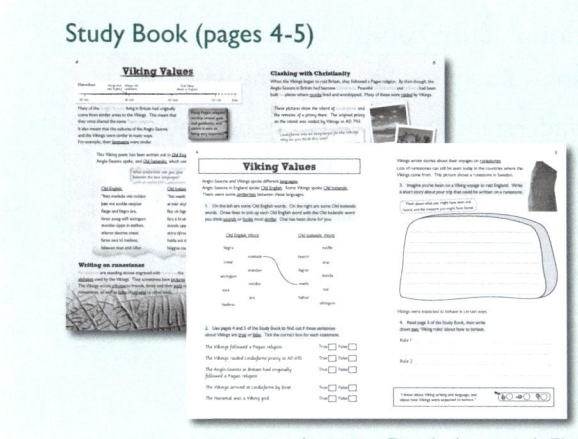

Activity Book (pages 4-5)

National Curriculum Aims
- Know about the history of the wider world.
- Understand similarity and difference and use them to draw contrasts.
- Create structured accounts.

Introduction

The poem on page 4 in the Study Book is an extract from Egil's Saga, an Icelandic narrative set between c. AD 850 and AD 1000. This is a modern translation of the extract: 'Thus counselled my mother / For me should they purchase / A galley and good oars / To go forth a-viking / So may I high-standing / A noble ship steering / Hold course for the haven / Hew down many foemen.' Sources like Egil's Saga demonstrate that the Vikings' values reflected their warrior culture, with courage and bravery being highly valued. However, they also reveal that etiquette and good manners were important to the Vikings, who were expected to show hospitality, courtesy and respect to others. Like the Anglo-Saxons, the Vikings were a Germanic people, and so the two groups shared a similar culture and language. After pupils have read pages 4-5 in the Study Book, ask them if they think the similarities between the Anglo-Saxons and the Vikings might have affected how easily the Vikings settled in Britain.

Answers to Activity Book Questions

1. fægra — fagrar / cnear — knerri / standan — standa / wícingum — víkingum / módor — móðir / swá — svá / ára — árar / hæfene — hafnar
2. True — False — True — True — False
3. Pupils should use the information on Viking raids on page 5 in the Study Book to write their story, as well as their own imaginations.
4. E.g. *Rule 1*: Always be honourable / truthful / brave. *Rule 2*: Have good manners.

Extra Activities

- Show pupils the above translation of the poem in the Study Book and ask them if they can work out the meaning of any of the Old English words (e.g. módor — mother, standan — standing). Then discuss with pupils which words they worked out and how they did it. Are they surprised that there are similarities in pronunciation and spelling between a language used over 1000 years ago and one we use today?

- Give pupils a copy of the Viking runic alphabet from the internet. Ask them to use the runic symbols to write out a short fact that they have learnt about the Vikings. Then get pupils to swap their fact with a partner, who should try to decipher what it says.

- Discuss with the class how we know the best way to behave today. How are the Vikings' rules about how to behave similar to today's rules? Or to school rules? Get pupils to write a set of rules for how they think they should behave on a daily basis. Discuss whether pupils think they follow the rules they have written.

- Ask pupils to look back at the extract from the Havamal on page 5 in the Study Book. Get pupils to write their own poem based on the rules of behaviour they came up with in the previous activity.

Norse Beliefs

Study Book (pages 6-7)

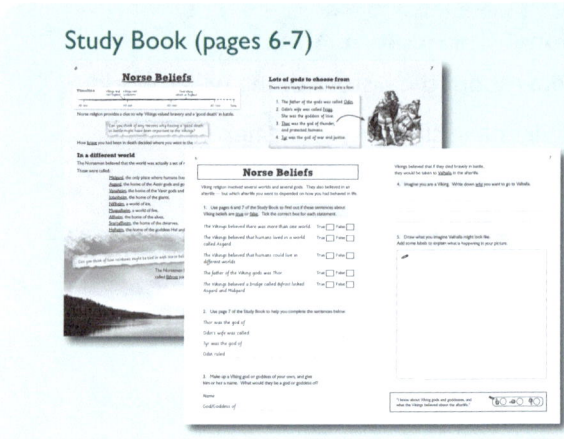

Activity Book (pages 6-7)

National Curriculum Aims

- Know about the history of the wider world.
- Understand the connections between religious and social history.
- Create structured accounts.

Introduction

The Vikings' Pagan religion was vastly different to the Christianity of the Anglo-Saxons. The Vikings believed in many gods and goddesses, as well as giants, elves and dwarves. We know a lot about these beliefs from Viking stories and poems, which describe the creation of the world right through to its destruction, and detail the adventures of the gods and goddesses. This ancient mythology still has a cultural influence on our world today, featuring in films, comics and books. After pupils have read pages 6-7 in the Study Book, ask them if they are familiar with any of the names mentioned there. Where have they heard them? What do they know about them?

Answers to Activity Book Questions

1. True — False — False — False — True

2. *Thor was the god of* thunder. *Odin's wife was called* Frigg. *Tyr was the god of* war and justice. *Odin ruled* Valhalla.

3. Any appropriate answer. Pupils should try to make a link between the name and what they are a god of, e.g. Everestina could be the goddess of mountains.

4. E.g. I want to go to Valhalla in the afterlife because there are feasts every day, and the food and drink never run out. I would be treated like a hero.

5. Pupils' drawings should show that Valhalla would have been a good place where the Vikings would have been happy. They may have drawn the Vikings eating and drinking at a feast.

Extra Activities

- Split pupils into groups and ask each group to research a Norse god or goddess, e.g. Thor, Odin, Loki, Frigg, Tyr, Balder, Freyja and Freyr. What were they god of? What special powers or weapons did they have? What was their relationship with other Norse deities? What stories and myths were told about them?

- Split pupils into nine groups and assign each group one of the nine worlds the Vikings believed in. Ask each group to draw their world on a large piece of paper. A class display can then be made from all the drawings.

- Ask pupils to write their own Norse myth. It could feature the god or goddess they came up with for question 3 and / or actual Norse gods. Get them to think about where their story is set — it could be in Midgard, Asgard or any of the other worlds the Vikings believed in. What happens in the myth — does the main character have to fight someone, rescue someone or go on a quest to find something?

- As a class, discuss why Valhalla appealed to the Vikings. What do pupils know about other religions' beliefs about the afterlife? Are they similar or different to the Vikings' beliefs? Why do pupils think that might be?

Discover & Learn British History — Vikings

Viking Voyages

Study Book (pages 8-9)

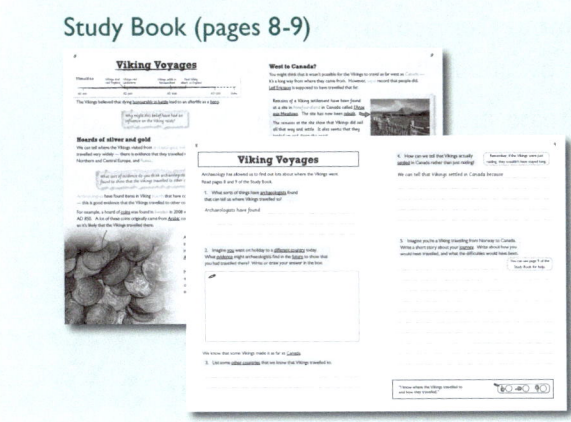

Activity Book (pages 8-9)

National Curriculum Aims
- Know about the history of the wider world.
- Understand how evidence is used to make historical claims.
- Create structured accounts.

Introduction

The Vikings were such successful travellers that they were probably the first Europeans to reach Canada and establish a settlement there. Having already settled in Iceland and Greenland, they then travelled even further west in the hope of finding fertile land and other natural resources. Canada didn't disappoint, but the Vikings' settlement at l'Anse aux Meadows was not permanent. It seems to have been used as a temporary base from which to explore, and was eventually abandoned completely for reasons which are still not fully understood.

Answers to Activity Book Questions

1. E.g. *Archaeologists have found* items in Viking hoards that come from different countries. For example, they have found foreign coins.

2. Pupils should list or draw relevant examples of things archaeologists might find, e.g. souvenirs, postcards with foreign stamps, passport stamps, boat, train and plane tickets, boarding passes.

3. E.g. England, Scotland, Ireland, Russia, Syria, Iraq

4. E.g. *We can tell that Vikings settled in Canada because* the remains of a settlement have been found on a site in Canada. Archaeologists have found items like pins, knitting needles and spindles there, which suggests women travelled there too.

5. Pupils should use information from page 9 in the Study Book, as well as their own imaginations. Their answers should show they understand that the journey would have been long and challenging.

Extra Activities

- Discuss with pupils the importance of critically evaluating evidence. Do they think that the items from different countries found in Viking hoards definitely prove that the Vikings travelled to those countries? Ask them to suggest other reasons why they might have been found there, e.g. foreign travellers coming to Scandinavia and trading the items there.

- Ask pupils to research Leif Ericsson (the Viking explorer who is believed to have been the first European to reach Canada) and write a biography of him. Pupils should include when and where he was born, his travels and exploits before he went to Canada and how he reached Canada.

- Ask pupils to research travel in Viking longships and produce a leaflet about it. How fast could longships travel? How many people could they carry? What was life like onboard? What were the Vikings' methods of navigation and how reliable were they? Pupils should also include a labelled map in their leaflet showing all the different countries the Vikings are thought to have travelled to.

Raiding and Trading

Study Book (pages 10-11)

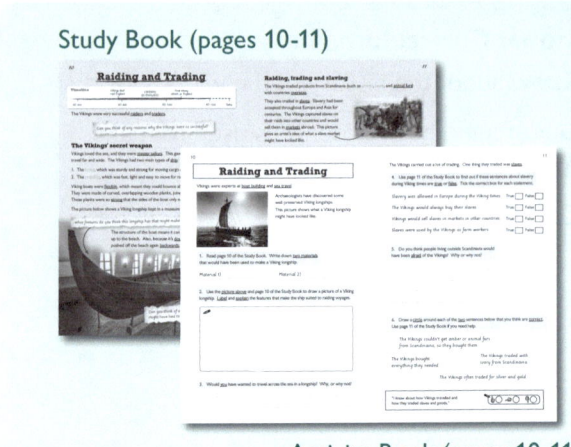

Activity Book (pages 10-11)

National Curriculum Aims
- Know about the history of the wider world.
- Create structured accounts.

Introduction

The Vikings embarked on raids to acquire riches and material goods, but they also used the more peaceful method of trading. In both areas, the Vikings showed skill and industry, and their success was underpinned by their impressive shipbuilding techniques. Fast, light longships enabled a quick getaway after raids, while strong knarrs could move heavy loads. The Vikings' remarkable aptitude for seafaring allowed them to build a vast trading network in Europe and beyond — by travelling across the Mediterranean and navigating Russian rivers, they even gained access to exotic goods like silk and spices from the east. The Vikings also traded slaves, so before pupils read page 11 in the Study Book, make sure they understand the concept of slavery.

Answers to Activity Book Questions

1. E.g. *Material 1)* wood   *Material 2)* iron
2. Pupils should have labelled and explained the key features of a longship. E.g. A sail to help the ship travel quickly using the wind. / A structure which allows it to be sailed in shallow water right up to the beach. / A double ended design which allows it to be pushed quickly off the beach backwards and rowed away to sea.
3. Pupils may answer either way, as long as they give a sensible reason to support their answer.
4. True — False — True — True
5. Pupils may answer either way, as long as they give a sensible reason to support their answer.
6. Pupils should have circled:
   The Vikings traded with ivory from Scandinavia.
   The Vikings often traded for silver and gold.

Extra Activities

- Ask pupils to imagine they are a Viking who is upgrading their boat. Get them to come up with some extra design features which would have made the Vikings' long sea journeys more comfortable. Pupils should draw their design and label it.
- Discuss with pupils why the Vikings travelled by sea. Show pupils maps and pictures of Scandinavia and encourage them to think about factors like terrain, climate, possible routes and the forms of land transport that were available to the Vikings. Why do they think sea travel was the best option for the Vikings?
- As a class, discuss the topic of slavery. What do pupils know about it? Explain that slavery was officially abolished in Britain in the nineteenth century, but that it still exists today in various forms. Are pupils surprised by this? How would pupils feel if they lost their freedom?

Viking Visits

Study Book (pages 12-13)

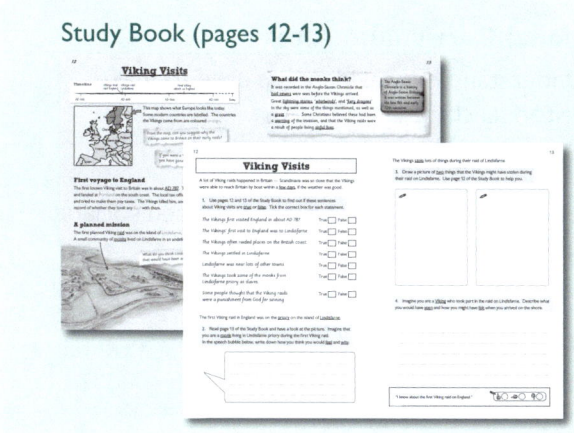

Activity Book (pages 12-13)

National Curriculum Aims

- Know and understand the history of Britain as a chronological narrative.
- Create structured accounts.
- Know how Britain has been influenced by the wider world.

Introduction

The Viking raid on the Christian priory of Lindisfarne in 793 was a worrying sign of what was to come for Britain's wealthy and largely undefended religious communities. The Vikings ransacked the monastery, taking valuables and holy objects, killing some monks on the spot and taking others prisoner. These brutal actions showed people in Britain how dangerous the Vikings could be. The attack was particularly shocking for the Anglo-Saxons because Lindisfarne was the base from which Christianity had been revived in northern England, and it had become one of the most important religious centres in the north. As Pagans, the Vikings had little respect for Christianity and, therefore, no qualms about attacking Christian monasteries. For them, raids such as the one on Lindisfarne served to enhance their reputations as warriors and improve their social status.

Answers to Activity Book Questions

1. True — False — True — False — False — True — True
2. Any appropriate answer. Pupils' answers should show an understanding that the Vikings posed a threat to the monks.
3. Pupils should have drawn any two of the things listed on page 12 in the Study Book (gold and silver treasures, plates, candlesticks, books).
4. Any appropriate answer. Pupils should have used information from pages 12-13 in the Study Book as well as their own imaginations.

Extra Activities

- Split the class into groups and ask them to plan and perform a television news item about the Lindisfarne attack. Their broadcast should include a newsreader reporting on the story, eye-witness accounts and a comment on the situation from a local leader.
- Split the class into pairs. One pupil should pretend to be a monk at Lindisfarne, and the other a Viking who raided the monastery. Get pupils to debate the attack in their pairs. How would the Viking justify his actions? How would the monk feel about the attack? How would he argue against the Viking's behaviour?
- Ask pupils to produce an informative poster about why the Vikings attacked Lindisfarne and why the attack was so successful, e.g. the monastery was very wealthy, it was close to the sea, it had no defences, it was isolated, the Vikings had ships which were adapted for raiding. They should use drawings and diagrams to present the information in an interesting and engaging way.

Discover & Learn British History — Vikings

Violent Vikings?

Study Book (pages 14-15)

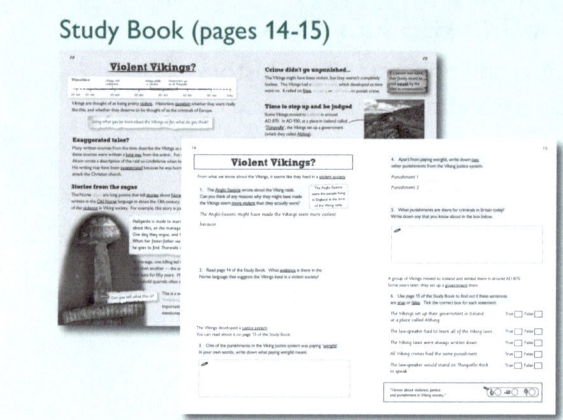

Activity Book (pages 14-15)

National Curriculum Aims

- Understand how evidence is used to make historical claims.
- Understand change.
- Understand the connections between social and political history.

Introduction

In popular culture, the Vikings have a reputation for being bloodthirsty brutes, raping and pillaging wherever they went. This view is supported by some historians, who portray the Vikings as mass murderers, guilty of committing numerous atrocities. Other historians, however, argue that this view of Viking violence is skewed because it prioritises eyewitness testimony from the victims of raids, who may have exaggerated the Vikings' brutality. These historians emphasise evidence for the Vikings' role as traders, sailors and craftsmen and suggest that the Vikings were no more violent than their contemporaries. After pupils have read pages 14-15 in the Study Book, ask them to write down their personal view of the Vikings in a few sentences.

Answers to Activity Book Questions

1. E.g. *The Anglo-Saxons might have made the Vikings seem more violent because* they might have been shocked that they would attack the Christian church and might have wanted to give the Vikings a bad name.

2. E.g. The sagas are stories written in the Norse language. They include descriptions of Viking violence. For example, in Njal's saga, one killing leads to another, then another.

3. E.g. If somebody was killed, their family would be paid wergild by the killer. This was money to compensate the family for their loss.

4. *Punishment 1* fines   *Punishment 2* outlawing

5. E.g. prison / fines / electronic tagging / community service

6. False — True — False — False — False

Extra Activities

- Ask pupils to share their answers to question 1 in the Activity Book and discuss why it is important to think about the reliability of sources. If we had sources written by Vikings about their raids, might those be biased too? In what ways? Can pupils think of any hypothetical examples of evidence that might be more reliable? E.g. photographs or a video taken during a Viking raid.

- Discuss with pupils how the Vikings' justice system compares with ours today. What are the similarities and differences? What do pupils think of wergild and outlawing? Would they have been fair and effective? Do they think our justice system is better or worse than the Vikings'?

- Get pupils to imagine they are a Viking involved with setting up the Althing in Iceland. Ask them to write a speech explaining to other Vikings what the government is and why it is being set up. Pupils could then perform their speeches to the rest of the class.

More Viking Visits

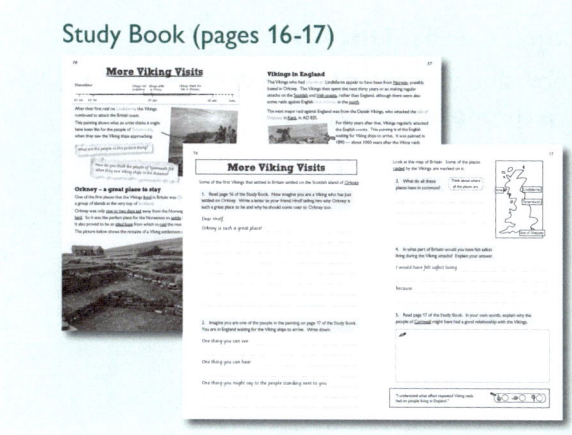

Study Book (pages 16-17)

Activity Book (pages 16-17)

National Curriculum Aims
- Know and understand the history of Britain as a chronological narrative.
- Create structured accounts.
- Understand connections between local and national history.

Introduction

The Vikings' raid on Lindisfarne was a watershed for Viking activity in Britain, and over the next few decades they regularly raided the British coast. For example, the abbey of Iona off the west coast of Scotland was repeatedly attacked, with 68 monks killed in a single raid. Monasteries in the north of England were destroyed and Ireland too was heavily targeted. Around this time, the Vikings also began to settle in Britain, and the isle of Orkney was the site for one of their first permanent footholds. It is uncertain whether they forcibly took land from the native Picts or integrated more peacefully, but over the next few generations the Vikings established themselves so well in Orkney that their culture and language became dominant there.

Answers to Activity Book Questions

1. Pupils' letters should mention that Orkney has plenty of land, is close to Norway and is in a convenient position for raiding other parts of Britain.

2. E.g. *One thing you can see*: Viking ships / Vikings
   One thing you can hear: the waves / people talking
   One thing you might say to the people standing next to you: "There are a lot of ships coming this way."

3. E.g. They're all around the coast of Britain.

4. E.g. *I would have felt safest living* in the middle of Britain, far away from the coast *because* the Vikings arrived by sea and raided places on the coast, so I'd be far away from them.

5. E.g. The people of Cornwall mined tin. This was something that the Vikings might have wanted to trade for, so it was a good idea for the Vikings to have a good relationship with the people in Cornwall.

Extra Activities

- Ask pupils to write a job description for a place on a Viking ship that is preparing to attack a coastal village in Britain. What does the job involve? What skills are needed? What are the benefits of this job for applicants?

- Get pupils to research the Brough of Birsay, a tidal island off Orkney where the Vikings settled. Ask them to make an informative poster which includes a drawing or diagram of the site. They should include information about the site's defensive features, the kind of dwellings the Vikings built, Viking leaders who lived there, artefacts that have been found and what can be seen there today.

- Ask pupils to look back at the paintings of Viking raids on pages 16 and 17 in the Study Book and to draw or paint their own version from the perspective of the arriving Vikings. As a class, discuss the differences between the pupils' pictures and those in the Study Book.

Discover & Learn British History — Vikings

Viking Victories

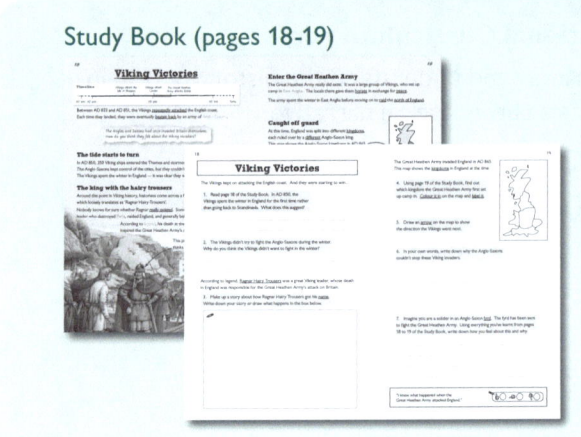

Study Book (pages 18-19)

Activity Book (pages 18-19)

National Curriculum Aims

- Know and understand the history of Britain as a chronological narrative.
- Create structured accounts.

Introduction

During the AD 850s and AD 860s, Viking activity in Britain evolved from seasonal raids to longer-term invasion and settlement. This shift is illustrated by the arrival of the Great Heathen Army in East Anglia in AD 865. Made up of different Viking war bands which had joined forces, this was the largest Viking army that had yet set foot in Britain. The Anglo-Saxons were ill-equipped to respond to this threat, since they had no standing army and their temporary forces, known as fyrds, took too long to mobilise. In addition, the Anglo-Saxons were accustomed to fighting short pitched battles, so they struggled to cope with the Vikings' tactic of attacking one place and then quickly moving on to another. Before pupils read pages 18-19 in the Study Book, ask them why they think the Vikings went from raiding to invading and settling.

Answers to Activity Book Questions

1. E.g. It suggests that the Vikings were getting stronger, and were able to fight off the Anglo-Saxons.
2. E.g. It would have been cold and there might not have been much food.
3. Any appropriate answer or drawing.
4. Pupils should have coloured in East Anglia on the map and labelled it.
5. Pupils should have drawn an arrow pointing north from East Anglia.
6. E.g. England at the time was split into several Anglo-Saxon kingdoms, which often argued. When the Vikings arrived, the Anglo-Saxons were too disorganised to fight together against them.
7. Any appropriate answer. Pupils might write that they feel scared / hopeless / frustrated because fyrds aren't an effective enough force to fight large numbers of Vikings.

Extra Activities

- Explain that some historians think Ragnar Lodbrok got his name because he wore trousers made from animal skin. Did pupils come up with a similar explanation for his name or did they have other ideas? Ask pupils to think about the meaning of the Viking name they gave themselves in the second Extra Activity on page 58. Get them to draw a picture of themselves which reflects that meaning.

- Ask pupils to pretend they are the leader of one of the Anglo-Saxon kingdoms. Get them to write a speech to persuade the kingdoms to work together to defeat the Vikings. Why would it be better to work together? What dangers do the Vikings pose to them?

- Get pupils to pretend they are a member of the Great Heathen Army in East Anglia and ask them to write a letter home to their family about the invasion of Britain. How do they think the invasion is going so far? Do they think they will be able to beat the Anglo-Saxons? What are they going to do next?

Discover & Learn British History — Vikings

Defeating the Anglo-Saxons

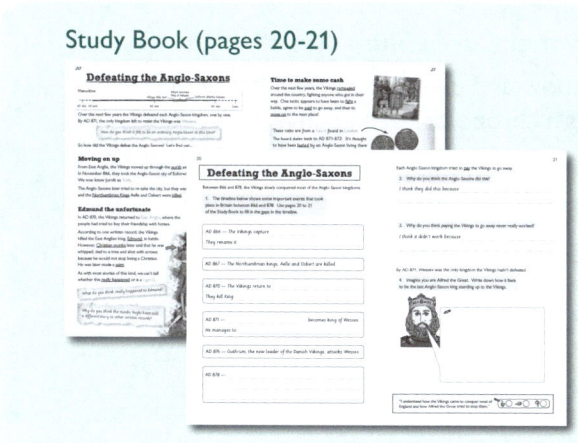

Study Book (pages 20-21)

Activity Book (pages 20-21)

National Curriculum Aims

- Know and understand the history of Britain as a chronological narrative.
- Create structured accounts.
- Understand cause and consequence.

Introduction

The arrival of the Great Heathen Army in AD 865 marked the beginning of the end for Anglo-Saxon control over many parts of England. From East Anglia, the army attacked Northumbria and Mercia, then returned to East Anglia, asserting their dominance over each of these Anglo-Saxon kingdoms as they went. However, Wessex did not fall so easily. Alfred, the king of Wessex, maintained an uneasy peace with the Vikings for several years. He was eventually forced to fight them after they began hostilities in AD 876, but although the Vikings eventually killed many of Alfred's men, they did not succeed in catching or killing Alfred himself, who fled to Somerset.

Answers to Activity Book Questions

1. E.g. AD 866 — *The Vikings capture* York. *They rename it* Jorvik.
   AD 870 — *The Vikings return to* East Anglia. *They kill King* Edmund.
   AD 871 — Alfred *becomes king of* Wessex. *He manages to* pay off the Vikings.
   AD 878 — The Vikings attack Alfred at Chippenham and kill many of his men. Alfred runs away to Somerset.

2. E.g. *I think they did this because* they hoped the Vikings would take the money and leave them alone.

3. E.g. *I think it didn't work because* the Vikings knew that if they came back they could get the Anglo-Saxons to pay them again.

4. Any appropriate answer. Pupils might write that they are worried the Vikings will completely take over the country, or that they are confident they can still beat the Vikings in battle.

Extra Activities

- Get pupils to look back at question 1 in the Activity Book and ask them to make a longer timeline of events involving the Vikings in Britain. They should start with the Viking raid on Lindisfarne in AD 793 and use the Study Book to find other events, such as the attack on the Isle of Sheppey in AD 835 and the arrival of the Great Heathen Army in AD 865. Pupils could also research other events such as the Viking raids on Iona.

- Ask pupils to imagine they are an advisor to an Anglo-Saxon king who is going to try and pay the Vikings to leave. Get pupils to write down other ways they could get the Vikings to leave and then discuss their ideas as a class.

- Split pupils into pairs. Ask one pupil in each pair to take on the role of a Viking and the other to take on the role of an Anglo-Saxon after Alfred's flight to Somerset in AD 878. Each pupil should explain their character's thoughts and feelings, e.g. the Viking might feel jubilant because they have won a victory over Alfred, but the Anglo-Saxon might feel angry because the Vikings have broken the peace again.

Discover & Learn British History — Vikings

Alfred the Great

Study Book (pages 22-23)

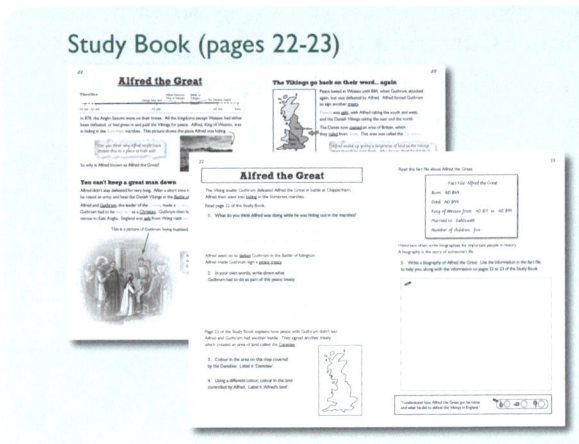

Activity Book (pages 22-23)

National Curriculum Aims

- Know and understand the history of Britain as a chronological narrative.
- Know how people's lives have shaped Britain.
- Create structured accounts.

Introduction

Alfred the Great managed to prevent the Vikings from gaining control over all of England. Although he fled to the Somerset marshes early in AD 878, he did not surrender. Instead, he conducted a guerrilla campaign until he was able to summon more troops for a full-scale battle. By May, Alfred's army was ready. His forces defeated the Vikings at Edington and forced them to retreat to their base in Chippenham where they were besieged. Two weeks later, the Vikings surrendered. This helped to restore Alfred's status as a strong leader, and he showed his strength again when he defeated another Viking attack in AD 884. Although the treaty that followed gave the Vikings a huge area of England, it also placed Alfred firmly in control of most of southern and western England. Determined that the Viking threat would be better met in future, Alfred then took measures to improve the Anglo-Saxons' fighting capabilities, both on land and on water.

Answers to Activity Book Questions

1. E.g. I think he was preparing his army for the next battle with the Vikings.
2. E.g. Guthrum had to be baptised as a Christian. He then had to leave Wessex and retreat back to East Anglia.
3. Pupils should have coloured and labelled the Danelaw.
4. Pupils should have coloured and labelled Alfred's land.
5. Any appropriate answer. Pupils should include information about Alfred from both the fact file and pages 22-23 in the Study Book.

Extra Activities

- Get pupils to research King Alfred and write a biography of him. When and where was he born? Who were his family members? What did he do before he became king? How did he become king? How did he deal with the Vikings? What did he achieve during peacetime? You could then make a class anthology of all the biographies.

- Ask pupils to think about how Guthrum might have felt after the first treaty with Alfred when he had to become a Christian and after the second treaty when the Danelaw was created. Get them to write two short diary entries describing Guthrum's thoughts and feelings.

- Get pupils to imagine they are King Alfred in the 880s. They should design a poster to publicise his plans to get England back on its feet again. It should explain what he plans to do (e.g. reorganise the army, change battle tactics, improve education) and why he wants to do these things. Then discuss with the class how they think the Anglo-Saxons might have reacted to Alfred's initiatives.

The Danes and the Danelaw

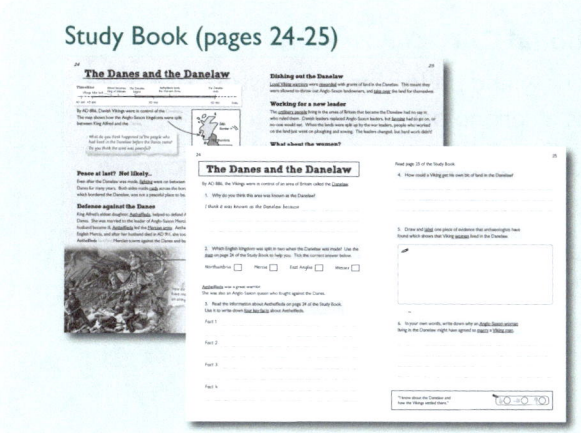

Study Book (pages 24-25)

Activity Book (pages 24-25)

National Curriculum Aims

- Know and understand the history of Britain as a chronological narrative.
- Understand how evidence is used to make historical claims.

Introduction

Under Alfred the Great, a boundary was drawn across England from London to Chester. The area north and east of this boundary was controlled by Danish Vikings and so it became known as the Danelaw. The Danes left their mark on this area and its people as they settled, farmed and traded there. Their Scandinavian language and culture influenced and mingled with those of the Anglo-Saxons, and the people themselves merged through marriage. This Viking influence can still be seen today in place names and in some English words. After pupils have read pages 24-25 in the Study Book, ask them to think about where they live — in the ninth century would they have been living in Northumbria, Mercia, East Anglia or Wessex? Would this have been in the Danelaw or in Alfred's land? Would pupils rather have lived in the Danelaw or in Alfred's land?

Answers to Activity Book Questions

1. E.g. *I think it was known as the Danelaw because* some of the Vikings came from Denmark and were called Danes. They controlled the law in that part of the land.

2. Pupils should have ticked: Mercia.

3. E.g. Aethelfleda was King Alfred's eldest daughter. / Aethelfleda was married to Aethelred. / Aethelfleda led the Mercian army. / Aethelfleda took charge of defence of English Mercia after her husband died.

4. E.g. Loyal warriors were rewarded with land. They were allowed to throw out the original Anglo-Saxon landowners and take over the land themselves.

5. Pupils should have drawn one or both of the Viking woman's brooches on page 25 in the Study Book.

6. E.g. If a woman's male relatives had died, she might struggle to support herself. If she married a Viking man, she would have some support, for example, somewhere to live and food to eat.

Extra Activities

- Ask pupils to find out more about Aethelfleda and create a poster about her achievements and how she was different from most women of her time. Then as a class, discuss the similarities and differences between the available information about Aethelfleda and King Alfred. Why do pupils think historians have more information about some people from history than they do about others?

- Get pupils to imagine that they are an Anglo-Saxon landowner who has been thrown off his land by a Viking. Ask them to write a letter to a friend explaining what happened and how they feel about it.

- Explain that the modern names of many places that were in the Danelaw have Scandinavian origins, e.g place names that end in '-thwaite', '-toft', '-keld', '-by' and '-kirk'. Get pupils to look at a map of England to see if they can spot any place names that have these endings. Are there any in the area where they live?

Discover & Learn British History — Vikings

Viking Jorvik

Study Book (pages 26-27)

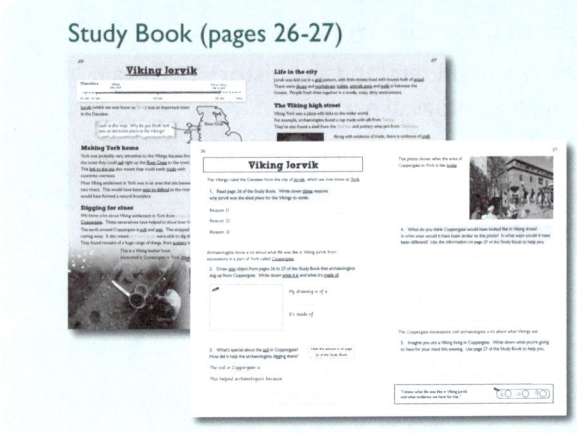

Activity Book (pages 26-27)

National Curriculum Aims

- Know and understand the history of Britain as a chronological narrative.
- Understand how evidence is used to make historical claims.
- Understand similarity and difference and use them to draw contrasts.

Introduction

York (Jorvik) had been an important settlement long before the Vikings arrived. Founded by the Romans as Eboracum in around AD 71, it became a major military, political and economic centre. After the Romans' departure, the Anglo-Saxons renamed the city Eoforwic and made it the capital of Northumbria. Under the Vikings, Eoforwic became Jorvik. It grew in size and its significance as a trading centre increased. Archaeological excavations in York have unearthed a wealth of information about the Vikings who lived there, and the city's Viking past is also evident in street names such as Coppergate, Goodramgate and Skeldergate — the ending 'gate' comes from the Viking word 'gata', meaning 'street'.

Answers to Activity Book Questions

1. E.g. They could sail right up the river from the sea. / They could use the river for trade. / The rivers would have made Jorvik easy to defend.
2. Pupils should have drawn any of the objects from pages 26-27 in the Study Book and written what it is and what it is made of.
3. *The soil in Coppergate is* wet and soft. *This helped archaeologists because* it stopped many items that were buried there from rotting away, and also meant that they could dig a long way down.
4. Any appropriate answer. Pupils should have made direct comparisons between modern-day Coppergate and Viking Coppergate.
5. Any appropriate answer. The meal should be made up of items listed on page 27 in the Study Book, or other foods that would have been available in Viking York.

Extra Activities

- Discuss with pupils the importance of archaeological excavations. Apart from the objects mentioned on pages 26-27 in the Study Book, what sorts of things from the Viking era do pupils think it would be useful to find? What would these objects tell them about what life was like for the Vikings? Are these things likely to be found? What kinds of things will we never be able to find out about the Vikings?
- Get pupils to find out more about what life was like for the Vikings in Jorvik. They should produce a poster to display their findings and present it to the class.
- Using the information from the Study Book and their own research, ask pupils to draw a scene from a street in Viking Jorvik. The drawings could then be collected and made into a class display.

Athelstan and Constantine

Study Book (pages 28-29)

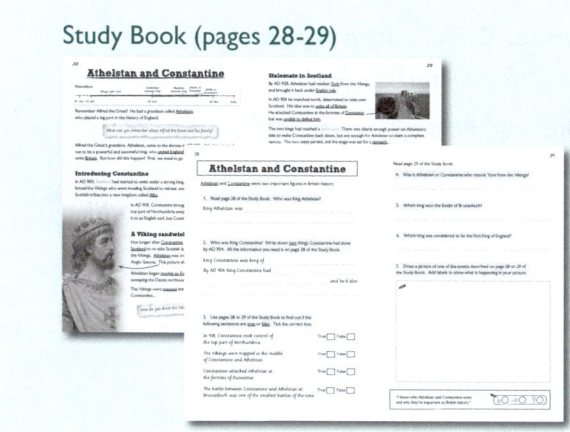

Activity Book (pages 28-29)

National Curriculum Aims

- Know and understand the history of Britain as a chronological narrative.
- Know how people's lives have shaped Britain.
- Understand cause and consequence.

Introduction

The Anglo-Saxon king Athelstan and the Scottish king Constantine II shared the aim of defeating the Vikings, and both won victories over them. However, while Constantine wanted to create a strong, united Scotland, Athelstan had the more ambitious vision of ruling over Scotland as part of a united Britain. In order to prevent this, Constantine joined forces with Olaf Guthfrithson, the Viking king of Dublin, and Owen, the king of Strathclyde, to launch an attack on Athelstan at Brunanburh. Athelstan won the battle, but the strength of the northern coalition's resistance put an end to his dream of ruling a united Britain. Some historians regard Brunanburh as one of the most important battles in Britain's history, arguing that it helped to establish England and Scotland as separate countries with distinct identities.

Answers to Activity Book Questions

1. E.g. *King Athelstan was* the grandson of King Alfred the Great, and he was king of England.
2. E.g. *King Constantine was king of* Scotland. *By AD 904 King Constantine had* forced the Vikings who were invading Scotland to retreat *and he'd also* started reorganising the Scottish tribes into one kingdom.
3. True — True — False — False
4. Athelstan
5. Athelstan
6. Athelstan
7. Any appropriate drawing. Pupils might have drawn Athelstan's army marching north to retake York from the Vikings, the battle at the fortress of Dunnottar or the Battle of Brunanburh. Their drawing should be labelled.

Extra Activities

- As a class, discuss why Athelstan and Constantine came into conflict. Ask pupils what else the two kings could have done instead of going to war, e.g. they could have held meetings and negotiated. Do they think this would have been effective? Do leaders in the modern world settle disputes in the way Athelstan and Constantine did, or do they use other methods?

- Ask pupils to imagine they are one of the people in the picture they drew for question 7 in the Activity Book. Get them to write a diary entry for the day shown in their picture.

- Ask pupils to do some research about the events before, during and after the Battle of Brunanburh. They should use their findings to write a newspaper article about the battle. Encourage them to include imagined reactions to the battle from both Vikings and Anglo-Saxons.

Vikings in the 10th Century

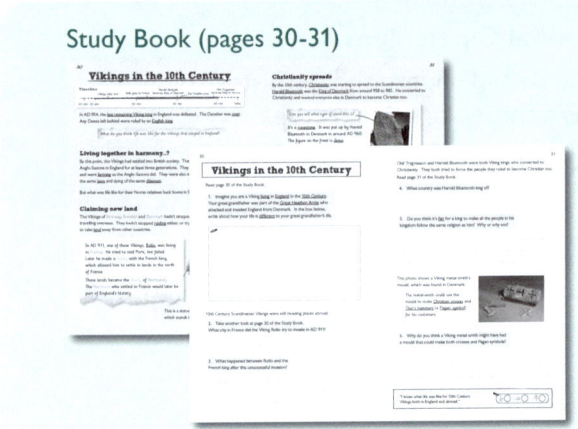

Study Book (pages 30-31)

Activity Book (pages 30-31)

National Curriculum Aims
- Create structured accounts.
- Understand similarity and difference and use them to draw contrasts.
- Know about the history of the wider world.
- Understand the connections between religious and social history.

Introduction

The power of the Vikings in England waned in the 10th century, with much of their land being taken back by the Anglo-Saxons. The last Viking king, Eric Bloodaxe of Jorvik, was driven out in AD 954, and this signalled the end of Viking rule. Vikings continued to live in England though — they had assimilated over the generations, adopting Anglo-Saxon language and culture, and even converting to Christianity. Unlike their counterparts in England, the Vikings living in Norway, Sweden and Denmark were still travelling and raiding, but they too began converting to Christianity. By the 10th century, the Church and Christian rulers were becoming increasingly powerful, so it served the political interests of the Vikings to be Christians too.

Answers to Activity Book Questions

1. Any appropriate answer. Pupils should highlight the fact that by the 10th century the Vikings were settled and living alongside the Anglo-Saxons rather than invading the land.
2. Paris
3. E.g. Rollo made an agreement with the French king and settled in lands in the north of France. These lands became the duchy of Normandy.
4. Denmark
5. Pupils may answer either way, as long as they give a sensible reason to support their answer.
6. E.g. The metal-smith might have lived in a place where people followed different religions. He could then make a cross or a hammer depending on what each customer wanted.

Extra Activities

- Get pupils to make an informative poster which charts the fortunes of the Vikings in Britain from their raid on Lindisfarne in AD 793 to the defeat of Eric Bloodaxe in AD 954. They should include these two events and choose at least five other key moments to cover. Encourage pupils to use drawings or diagrams in their poster.

- Ask for volunteers to explain to the class why they like their favourite book, film or band. The rest of the class should make arguments to try to persuade them to change their mind. Are these arguments effective? Why or why not? Discuss with pupils the conversion of the Vikings to Christianity. Do they think it would have been easy to persuade the Vikings to change their religion? Why or why not?

- Explain to pupils that the runestone mentioned on page 31 in the Study Book is called the Jelling Stone. It was put up by King Harald Bluetooth to celebrate his achievements, including the introduction of Christianity to Denmark. Get pupils to think of a time when they achieved something they were proud of. Ask them to design a runestone of their own which celebrates this achievement.

Aethelred is Unready!

Study Book (pages 32-33)

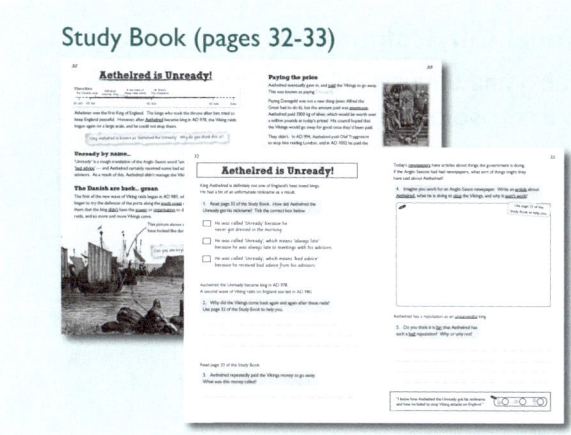

Activity Book (pages 32-33)

National Curriculum Aims

- Know and understand the history of Britain as a chronological narrative.
- Create structured accounts.
- Know how people's lives have shaped Britain.

Introduction

The end of Viking rule in England did not mean the end of Viking activity there. In AD 980, the Danes began to raid England yet again, and this time the Viking groups were better organised and headed by more powerful leaders. In AD 991, for example, Olaf Tryggvason brought 93 ships to raid the town of Maldon in Essex. To make matters worse, England was already militarily and politically weakened — King Aethelred seems to have been an ineffective general, he received poor counsel from his advisors, and his leadership was further undermined by divisions in the nobility. As a result, Aethelred's response to the Viking raids was inadequate and some of his tactics, such as ordering the massacre of all Danish men in England in 1002, created more problems than they solved.

Answers to Activity Book Questions

1. Pupils should have ticked: He was called 'Unready', which means 'bad advice' because he received bad advice from his advisors.

2. E.g. It became clear to the Vikings that Aethelred didn't have the power or the organisation to defend England against their raids.

3. Danegeld

4. Any appropriate answer. Pupils should use as much information from pages 32-33 in the Study Book as possible, as well as their own imaginations.

5. Pupils may answer either way, as long as they give a sensible reason to support their answer.

Extra Activities

- Ask pupils to research Aethelred and produce a fact sheet about him. Then discuss their findings as a class. Do they think it is fair that he has been judged so negatively by history? If they were in his position, what might they have done differently?

- Discuss Aethelred the Unready's nickname with pupils. Get them to come up with an original nickname for another king mentioned in the Study Book which reflects his actions or personality. Pupils can then share the name they have come up with and the reasons behind it with the rest of the class.

- Get pupils to imagine they are King Aethelred and that they have just read the article pupils wrote for question 4 in the Activity Book. Ask them to write King Aethelred's response to the article.

- Split pupils into pairs. Ask one pupil in each pair to take on the role of Aethelred and the other to take on the role of a Viking leader. Get pupils to pretend they are having a meeting to discuss the St Brice's Day massacre. What might Aethelred say to defend his actions? How might the Viking leader be feeling?

King Canute and Emma

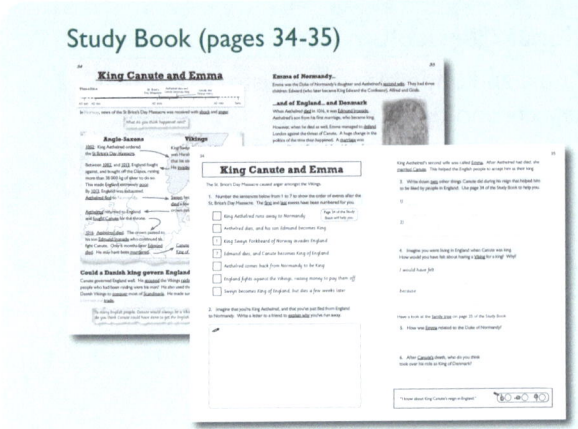

Study Book (pages 34-35)

Activity Book (pages 34-35)

National Curriculum Aims
- Know and understand the history of Britain as a chronological narrative.
- Create structured accounts.
- Understand change.

Introduction

The Vikings responded to the St Brice's Day massacre by intensifying their attacks on England. These attacks culminated in Sweyn Forkbeard's successful invasion of 1013, when he drove Aethelred into exile and took the crown for himself. England was once more under Viking rule, and although Forkbeard's reign only lasted for a few weeks, his son Canute was king for almost 20 years. Canute took several measures to gain acceptance from his Anglo-Saxon subjects. He was a generous supporter of the English Church and his laws were based on those of King Edgar, an Anglo-Saxon king whose reign was widely regarded as peaceful and successful. Perhaps most significantly, Canute married Emma of Normandy, a match which not only helped him gain acceptance, but also had major implications for the direction of British history. After pupils have read pages 34-35 in the Study Book, ask them how they think Emma might have felt about marrying a Viking. Why might she have agreed to do so?

Answers to Activity Book Questions

1. 3 — 6 — 1 — 7 — 5 — 2 — 4
2. Any appropriate answer. Pupils should use as much information from pages 34-35 in the Study Book as possible, as well as their own imaginations.
3. E.g. Canute stopped the Vikings raiding. / He made sure that Britain was involved in international trade.
4. Any appropriate answer. Pupils should give a sensible reason to support their answer.
5. E.g. She was his daughter. / He was her father.
6. Harthacnut

Extra Activities

- Ask pupils to look back at question 1 on page 34 in the Activity Book, and get them to create a storyboard of these events made up of 7 frames. When they have finished, ask pupils to cut out each frame in their storyboard and pass them to a partner who should try to arrange them in the correct order.

- Get pupils to pretend they are an Anglo-Saxon living during the reign of King Canute. Ask them to write a letter to a friend, telling them what they think of Canute and how he compares to Aethelred. Do they prefer Canute or Aethelred? Why?

- Show the class the eleventh-century illustrations of Emma of Normandy from the New Minster *Liber Vitae* and the *Encomium Emmae Reginae*. Ask pupils to draw their own picture of Emma in the same style. They should write a short biography to accompany their drawing, covering the key events in Emma's life.

- Ask pupils to look back at the family tree on page 35 in the Study Book, then get them to draw their own family tree. They could decorate it with drawings of their family members.

The Kings After Canute

Study Book (pages 36-37)

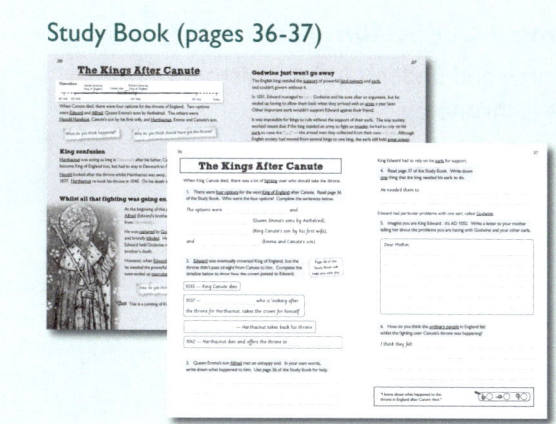

Activity Book (pages 36-37)

National Curriculum Aims

- Know and understand the history of Britain as a chronological narrative.
- Create structured accounts.
- Understand change.
- Understand the connections between political and social history.

Introduction

Canute wasn't just king of England — he also ruled Denmark, Norway and parts of Sweden. After his death in AD 1035, however, his heirs did not enjoy such successful reigns, and Canute's North Sea Empire rapidly crumbled. In England, the throne eventually passed back into Anglo-Saxon hands when Edward, Aethelred's son by Emma, became king in 1042. Edward's reign was relatively successful, but his power was constantly challenged by Earl Godwine of Wessex, one of the most powerful men in England after the king himself. Before pupils read pages 36-37 in the Study Book, it may be helpful for them to look back at the family tree on page 35 to ensure they know who all the key figures are and how they are related to one another.

Answers to Activity Book Questions

1. *The options were* Edward *and* Alfred *(Queen Emma's sons by Aethelred),* Harold Harefoot *(King Canute's son by his first wife) and* Harthacnut *(Emma and Canute's son).*

2. *1037 —* Harold, *who is looking after the throne for Harthacnut, takes the crown for himself.*
   1040 — Harthacnut takes back his throne.
   1042 — Harthacnut dies and offers the throne to *Edward.*

3. E.g. Alfred was captured by Godwine, the Earl of Wessex. He was blinded and died from his wounds.

4. E.g. *He needed them to* collect together the men for the fyrd / army.

5. Any appropriate answer. Pupils should use as much information from pages 36-37 in the Study Book as possible.

6. Any appropriate answer. Pupils might write that they were bored of the arguments because they were more concerned with trying to support their families, or angry because they didn't have a say in who would be king.

Extra Activities

- Split the class into groups and ask the pupils in each group to take on the roles of King Canute, Queen Emma, Aethelred, Edward, Alfred, Harold Harefoot and Harthacnut. As their characters, pupils should take it in turns to explain who they are, their relationship to the other characters and what happened to them.

- Ask pupils to look back at the letter they wrote for question 5 in the Activity Book. Get them to imagine they are Edward's mother and write a response telling Edward what he should do and why.

- As a class, discuss Edward's marriage to Edith. Given the troubled relationship between the two families, how do pupils think Edward and Edith might have felt about getting married? Do pupils think that it is fair to make people marry for political reasons?

The Conqueror is Coming

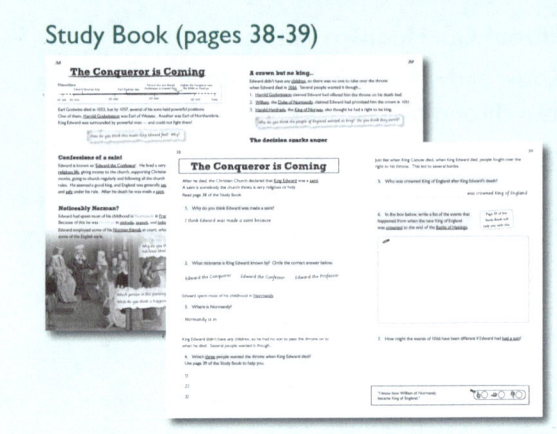

Study Book (pages 38-39)

Activity Book (pages 38-39)

National Curriculum Aims

- Know and understand the history of Britain as a chronological narrative.
- Understand change.
- Understand cause and consequence.

Introduction

When King Edward died, Harold Godwineson, one of the sons of Godwine, was crowned king of England. However, he immediately faced challenges to his crown from King Harald Hardrada of Norway and Duke William of Normandy. It was William who eventually emerged victorious, beating Harold at the Battle of Hastings in 1066. Although the Normans had Viking origins, by the mid-eleventh century they were firmly established in their duchy in northern France and had begun to develop a distinct cultural identity. Therefore, William of Normandy's accession to the English throne brought Viking and Anglo-Saxon rule in England to an end and marked the start of a new era in English history. Before pupils read pages 38-39 in the Study Book, it may be useful to show them where Normandy is on a map.

Answers to Activity Book Questions

1. E.g. *I think Edward was made a saint because* he lived a very religious life. He gave money to the church and supported monks, as well as going to church regularly.
2. Pupils should have circled: Edward the Confessor.
3. *Normandy is in* France.
4. Harold Godwineson / William, the Duke of Normandy / Harald Hardrada
5. Harold Godwineson *was crowned king of England*.
6. E.g. William was angry that Harold had been crowned and began building ships to invade Britain. Harald Hardrada invaded, and King Harold fought him at Stamford Bridge. Harald Hardrada was killed. William then invaded, and King Harold fought him at the Battle of Hastings. Harold was killed.
7. Any appropriate answer.

Extra Activities

- Ask pupils to research the Battle of Hastings and produce an informative poster about it, covering topics like when and where it happened, how many soldiers fought on each side and how William defeated Harold.
- Show pupils some pictures of the Bayeux Tapestry and ask them to find out more about it. They could then choose an event they have learnt about in the Study Book and draw a picture depicting it in the style of the Bayeux Tapestry. Get pupils to show their drawings to the rest of the class who should guess what they show.
- Split the class into groups and assign each group a topic from the Vikings Study Book. Ask each group to prepare a presentation on their topic which they will then present to the rest of the class. Pupils should use information from the Study Book in their presentations, as well as their own research.